A Research Guide to

Modern Irish Dramatists

A Research Guide to
Modern Irish Dramatists

by

E. H. Mikhail

The Whitston Publishing Company
Troy, New York
1979

Library of Congress Catalog Card Number 78-69874

ISBN 0-87875-166-1

Printed in the United States of America

LC 78069874

CONTENTS

Acknowledgements

It is a pleasant duty to record my appreciation to the staff of the University of Lethbridge Library; the British Library, London; the National Library of Ireland, Dublin; Trinity College Library, Dublin; the British Theatre Institute Library, London; and the New York Public Library.

Thanks are also due to Miss Bea Ramtej for her patience and skill in typing and preparing the final manuscript.

Preface

This is a bibliography of bibliographies of one hundred and two Irish dramatists who wrote from the beginning of the Irish Dramatic Movement in 1899 to the present time. I have compiled it in order to assist scholars and students of Modern Irish Drama in finding the most reliable bibliographical information on the dramatists of the period. Because only better-known playwrights have recently been the subject of bibliographical studies, I have included in this volume *all* the modern Irish dramatists—ranging from J. M. Synge and Sean O'Casey to the lesser-known Seamus Byrne and Frank Carney. Even those authors who wrote only one play have been listed.

The annotations are not evaluative, but descriptive and indicative of the content of the material they describe. Thus "Primary" signifies that the bibliography or checklist includes all the writings *by* the author, whether books or periodical contributions. "Primary First Editions" shows that all first editions or first publications are included, but not reprints or later editions. "Primary Books" indicates that no other form is included. "Secondary" means that the compiler has attempted to list all writings *about* the author, while "Secondary Selected" designates that the compiler has consciously omitted some writings.

I have attempted to make this *Guide* complete until the end of 1975, although some later entries have been included.

E. H. Mikhail

BECKETT, Samuel (1906-   )

Adelman, Irving, and Rita Dworkin. *Modern Drama; A Checklist of Critical Literature on 20th Century Plays* (Metuchen, New Jersey: Scarecrow Press, 1967), pp. 44-50 [Secondary selected].

Breed, Paul F., and Florence M. Sniderman. *Dramatic Criticism Index; A Bibliography of Commentaries on Playwrights from Ibsen to the Avant-Garde* (Detroit, Michigan: Gale Research Company, 1972), pp. 74-79 [Secondary selected].

Bryer, Jackson R. "Samuel Beckett: A Checklist of Criticism," *Samuel Beckett Now,* ed. Melvin J. Friedman (Chicago and London: University of Chicago Press, 1970), pp. 219-259.

Cohn, Ruby. "A Checklist of Beckett Criticism," *Perspective* (Washington University), XI (Autumn 1959), pp. 193-196.

Coleman, Arthur, and Gary R. Tyler. *Drama Criticism, Vol. 2: A Checklist of Interpretation Since 1940 of Classical and Continental Plays* (Chicago: Swallow Press, 1971), pp. 48-57 [Secondary selected].

Doherty, Francis. *Samuel Beckett* (London: Hutchinson University Library, 1971), pp. 153-154 [Secondary selected].

Duckworth, Colin. *Angels of Darkness; Dramatic Effect in Samuel Beckett* (London: George Allen & Unwin, 1972), pp. 146-147 [Secondary selected].

Ebert, Harold. "Literaturnachweis," *Samuel Becketts Dramaturgie der Ungewissheit* (Wien-Stuttgart: Wilhelm

Braumuller, 1974), pp. 159-163 [Primary books. Secondary selected].

Federman, Raymond, and John Fletcher. *Samuel Beckett; His Works and His Critics: An Essay in Bibliography* (Berkeley and London: University of California Press, 1970) [Primary and secondary].

Fletcher, John, and John Spurling. "Bibliographical Note," *Beckett; A Study of His Plays* (London: Eyre Methuen, 1972), pp. 147-149 [Primary and secondary selected].

Foucré, Michèle. "Bibliographie," *Le Geste et la Parole dans le Théâtre de Samuel Beckett* (Paris: Editions A.-G. Nizet, 1970), pp. 149-152 [Secondary selected].

Hagberg, Per Olof. "Bibliography," *The Dramatic Works of Samuel Beckett and Harold Pinter* (Gothenburg: University of Gothenburg, 1972), pp. 154-162 [First productions. Primary and secondary selected].

Kersnowski, Frank L., C. W. Spinks, and Laird Loomis. *A Bibliography of Modern Irish and Anglo-Irish Literature* (San Antonio, Texas: Trinity University Press, 1976), pp. 1-4 [Primary and secondary books].

Knowlson, James. "Beckett and the Theatre," *Samuel Beckett: An Exhibition Held at Reading University Library, May to July 1971* (London: Turret Books, 1971), pp. 60-106 [Manuscripts, theatre programmes, first productions, and primary books].

Mays, James. "Samuel Beckett Bibliography: Comments and Corrections," *Irish University Review* (Dublin), II, No. 2 (Autumn 1972), pp. 189-207 [Supplements Federman and Fletcher].

Mellown, Elgin W. *A Descriptive Catalogue of the Bibliographies of 20th Century British Poets, Novelists, and Dramatists* (Troy, New York: Whitston Publishing Company, 1978), pp. 17-18 [Primary and secondary bibliographies].

Palmer, Helen H., and Anne Jane Dyson. *European Drama Criticism* (Hamden, Connecticut: Shoe String Press, 1968), pp. 40-46; *Supplement I* (1970), pp. 14-20; *Supplement II* (1974), pp. 10-14 [Secondary selected].

Pilling, John. *Samuel Beckett* (London and Boston: Routledge & Kegan Paul, 1976), pp. 225-235 [Primary. Secondary selected and annotated].

Reid, Alec. *All I Can Manage, More Than I Could: An Approach to the Plays of Samuel Beckett* (Dublin: Dolmen Press; Chester Springs, Pennsylvania: Dufour Editions, 1968) [Contains a chronology of the plays, including dates of production].

Salem, James M. *A Guide to Critical Reviews, Part III: British and Continental Drama from Ibsen to Pinter* (Metuchen, New Jersey: Scarecrow Press, 1968), pp. 31-33 [Secondary periodicals].

Samples, Gordon. *The Drama Scholars' Index to Plays and Filmscripts; A Guide to Plays and Filmscripts in Selected Anthologies, Series and Periodicals* (Metuchen, New Jersey: Scarecrow Press, 1974), p. 32 [Primary].

Sen, Supti. *Samuel Beckett; His Mind and Art* (Calcutta: Firma K. L. Mukhopadhyay, 1970), pp. 204-212 [Primary and secondary selected].

Tanner, James T. F., and J. Don Vann. *Samuel Beckett: A Checklist of Criticism* (Kent: Kent State University, 1969) [Secondary selected].

Temple, Ruth Z., and Martin Tucker. *Twentieth Century British Literature: A Reference Guide and Bibliography* (New York: Frederick Ungar, 1968), p. 133 [Primary books].

Ventimiglia, Dario. *Il Teatro di Samuel Beckett* (Padova: Liviana Editrice, 1973), pp. 193-202 [Primary and secondary selected].

Webb, Eugene. "Critical Writings on Samuel Beckett: A Bibliography," *West Coast Review*, I (Spring 1966), pp. 56-70.

—. *The Plays of Samuel Beckett* (London: Peter Owen, 1972), pp. 149-150 [First productions] ; pp. 151-155 [Primary books. Secondary selected] .

Worth, Katharine J. "Samuel Beckett," *The New Cambridge Bibliography of English Literature, Vol. 4: 1900-1950*, ed. I. R. Willison (Cambridge: Cambridge University Press, 1972), columns 885-906 [Primary. Secondary selected] .

—, ed. *Beckett the Shape Changer; A Symposium* (London and Boston: Routledge & Kegan Paul, 1975), pp. 219-221 "Select List of Beckett's Principal Works"; pp. 223-224 "Select List of Critical Writings".

BEHAN, Brendan (1923-1964)

Adelman, Irving, and Rita Dworkin. *Modern Drama; A Checklist of Critical Literature on 20th Century Plays* (Metuchen, New Jersey: The Scarecrow Press, 1967), p. 50 [Secondary selected] .

"Books by Brendan Behan," *The Hollins Critic* (Hollins College, Virginia), II, No. 1 (February 1965), p. 7.

Boyle, Ted E. "Selected Bibliography," *Brendan Behan* (New York: Twayne Publishers, 1969), pp. 143-145 [Primary books. Secondary selected] .

Breed, Paul F., and Florence M. Sniderman. *Dramatic Criticism Index; A Bibliography of Commentaries on Playwrights from Ibsen to the Avant-Garde* (Detroit, Michigan: Gale Research Company, 1972), pp. 97-98 [Secondary selected] .

Coleman, Arthur, and Gary R. Tyler. *Drama Criticism, Vol.*

I: A Checklist of Interpretation Since 1940 of English and American Plays (Denver, Colorado: Alan Swallow, 1966), p. 30 [Secondary selected].

Kersnowski, Frank L., C. W. Spinks, and Laird Loomis. *A Bibliography of Modern Irish and Anglo-Irish Literature* (San Antonio, Texas: Trinity University Press, 1976), pp. 4-5 [Primary and secondary books].

Mellown, Elgin W. *A Descriptive Catalogue of the Bibliographies of 20th Century British Poets, Novelists, and Dramatists* (Troy, New York: Whitston Publishing Company, 1978), p. 21 [Primary and secondary bibliographies].

Mikhail, E. H. *Brendan Behan; An Annotated Bibliography of Criticism* (London: Macmillan, in the press).

Palmer, Helen H., and Anne Jane Dyson. *European Drama Criticism* (Hamden, Connecticut: Shoe String Press, 1968), pp. 47-48; *Supplement I* (1970), p. 20; *Supplement II* (1974), p. 14 [Secondary selected].

Porter, Raymond J. "Selected Bibliography," *Brendan Behan* (New York and London: Columbia University Press, 1973), p. 48 [Primary books. Secondary selected].

Salem, James M. *A Guide to ·Critical Reviews, Part III: British and Continental Drama from Ibsen to Pinter* (Metuchen, New Jersey: Scarecrow Press, 1968), pp. 34-35 [Secondary periodicals].

Samples, Gordon. *The Drama Scholars' Index to Plays and Filmscripts: A Guide to Plays and Filmscripts in Selected Anthologies, Series and Periodicals* (Metuchen, New Jersey: Scarecrow Press, 1974), p. 33 [Primary].

Temple, Ruth Z., and Martin Tucker. *Twentieth Century British Literature: A Reference Guide and Bibliography* (New York: Frederick Ungar, 1968), pp. 133-134 [Primary books].

**BIRMINGHAM, George A. [Canon James Owen Hannay]
(1865-1950)**

Mellown, Elgin W. *A Descriptive Catalogue of the Bibliographies of 20th Century British Poets, Novelists, and
Dramatists* (Troy, New York: Whitston Publishing Company, 1978), p. 29 [Primary and secondary bibliogra-
phies].

Nicoll, Allardyce. *English Drama 1900-1930; The Beginnings
of the Modern Period* (Cambridge: Cambridge University
Press, 1973), p. 512 [First productions].

Who Was Who 1941-1950, 4th ed. (London: Adam & Charles
Black; New York: St. Martin's Press, 1967), pp. 496-
497 [Primary books].

Willison, I. R., ed. "George A. Birmingham," *The New Cambridge Bibliography of English Literature, Vol. 4: 1900-
1950* (Cambridge: Cambridge University Press, 1972),
columns 529-530 [Primary books].

BOYLE, William (1853-1922)

Breed, Paul F., and Florence M. Sniderman. *Dramatic Criticism Index; A Bibliography of Commentaries on Playwrights from Ibsen to the Avant-Garde* (Detroit, Michigan: Gale Research Company, 1972), p. 116 [Secondary
selected].

Mac Namara, Brinsley, ed. *Abbey Plays 1899-1948* (Dublin:
At the Sign of the Three Candles, [1949]) [Productions
at the Abbey Theatre].

Mellown, Elgin W. *A Descriptive Catalogue of the Bibli-*

ographies of 20th Century British Poets, Novelists, and Dramatists (Troy, New York: Whitston Publishing Company, 1978), p. 36 [Primary and secondary bibliographies] .

Nicoll, Allardyce. *English Drama 1900-1930; The Beginnings of the Modern Period* (Cambridge: Cambridge University Press, 1973), p. 524 [First productions] .

Watson, George, ed. *The New Cambridge Bibliography of English Literature, Vol. 3: 1800-1900* (Cambridge: Cambridge University Press, 1969), column 1939 [Primary books] .

BYRNE, Seamus (1904-1968)

Hogan, Robert. *After the Irish Renaissance; A Critical History of the Irish Drama Since 'The Plough and the Stars'* (Minneapolis: University of Minnesota Press, 1967; London: Macmillan, 1968), p. 261 [Primary] ; pp. 74-76 [Criticism] .

CAMPBELL, Joseph [Seosamb MacCathmhaoil] (1879-1944)

Hogan, Robert. "The Modern Drama," *Anglo-Irish Literature: A Review of Research*, ed. Richard J. Finneran (New York: Modern Language Association, 1976), pp. 540-541 [Primary. Secondary selected] .

Kersnowski, Frank L., C. W. Spinks, and Laird Loomis. *A Bibliography of Modern Irish and Anglo-Irish Literature* (San Antonio, Texas: Trinity University Press, 1976), pp. 10-11 [Primary books] .

Mac Namara, Brinsley, ed. *Abbey Plays 1899-1948* (Dublin:

At the Sign of the Three Candles, [1949]) [Productions at the Abbey Theatre] .

Mellown, Elgin W. *A Descriptive Catalogue of the Bibliographies of 20th Century British Poets, Novelists, and Dramatists* (Troy, New York: Whitston Publishing Company, 1978), p. 53 [Primary bibliographies] .

Nicoll, Allardyce. *English Drama 1900-1930; The Beginnings of the Modern Period* (Cambridge: Cambridge University Press, 1973), p. 546 [First productions] .

O'Hegarty, Patrick Sarsfield. *A Bibliography of Joseph Campbell* (Dublin: Privately printed, 1940). Reprinted from *The Dublin Magazine,* XV (October-December 1940), pp. 58-61 [Primary books] .

CARNEY, Frank (1902-   )

Hogan, Robert. *After the Irish Renaissance; A Critical History of the Irish Drama Since 'The Plough and the Stars'* (Minneapolis: University of Minnesota Press, 1967; London: Macmillan, 1968), p. 261 [Primary books] .

Mac Namara, Brinsley, ed. *Abbey Plays 1899-1948* (Dublin: At the Sign of the Three Candles, [1949]) [Productions at the Abbey Theatre] .

CARROLL, Paul Vincent (1900-1968)

Adelman, Irving, and Rita Dworkin. *Modern Drama; A Checklist of Critical Literature on 20th Century Plays* (Metuchen, New Jersey: Scarecrow Press, 1967), p. 73 [Secondary selected] .

Breed, Paul F., and Florence M. Sniderman. *Dramatic Criticism Index; A Bibliography of Commentaries on Playwrights from Ibsen to the Avant-Garde* (Detroit, Michigan: Gale Research Company, 1972), pp. 147-148 [Secondary selected].

Doyle, Paul A. *Paul Vincent Carroll* (Lewisburg: Bucknell University Press, 1971), pp. 111-115 [Primary. Secondary selected].

Mac Namara, Brinsley, ed. *Abbey Plays 1899-1948* (Dublin: At the Sign of the Three Candles, [1949]) [Productions at the Abbey Theatre].

Mellown, Elgin W. *A Descriptive Catalogue of the Bibliographies of 20th Century British Poets, Novelists, and Dramatists* (Troy, New York: Whitston Publishing Company, 1978), pp. 55-56 [Primary and secondary bibliographies].

Moses, Montrose J., and Oscar J. Campbell, eds. *Dramas of Modernism and Their Forerunners* (Boston: Little Brown, 1941), pp. 933-934, 945 [Primary and secondary selected].

Palmer, Helen H., and Anne Jane Dyson. *European Drama Criticism* (Hamden, Connecticut: Shoe String Press, 1968), pp. 77-79 [Secondary selected].

Salem, James M. *A Guide to Critical Reviews. Part III; British and Continental Drama from Ibsen to Pinter* (Metuchen, New Jersey: Scarecrow Press, 1968), pp. 58-60 [Secondary selected].

Samples, Gordon. *The Drama Scholars' Index to Plays and Filmscripts; A Guide to Plays and Filmscripts in Selected Anthologies, Series and Periodicals* (Metuchen, New Jersey: Scarecrow Press, 1974), p. 61 [Primary selected].

Temple, Ruth Z., and Martin Tucker. *Twentieth Century British Literature: A Reference Guide and Bibliography* (New York: Frederick Ungar, 1968), p. 144 [Primary books].

Willison, I. R., ed. *The New Cambridge Bibliography of English Literature, Vol. 4: 1900-1950* (Cambridge: Cambridge University Press, 1972), columns 921-922 [Primary books. Secondary selected] .

CASEY, W[illiam] F[rancis] (-   )

Mac Namara, Brinsley, ed. *Abbey Plays 1899-1948* (Dublin: At the Sign of the Three Candles, [1949]) [Productions at the Abbey Theatre] .

Malone, Andrew E. *The Irish Drama* (London: Constable; New York: Scribner's, 1929), p. 336 [First productions] ; p. 235 [Criticism] .

Nicoll, Allardyce. *English Drama 1900-1930; The Beginnings of the Modern Period* (Cambridge: Cambridge University Press, 1973), pp. 552-553 [First productions] .

Robinson, Lennox. *Ireland's Abbey Theatre; A History 1899-1951* (London: Sidgwick & Jackson, 1951), pp. 81-82 [First productions] ; p. 59 [Criticism] .

CHEASTY, James (-   )

Hogan, Robert. *After the Irish Renaissance; A Critical History of the Irish Drama Since 'The Plough and the Stars'* (Minneapolis: University of Minnesota Press, 1967; London: Macmillan, 1968), p. 261 [Primary books] , p. 229 [Criticism] .

CLARKE, Austin (1896-1974)

Coleman, Arthur, and Gary R. Tyler. *Drama Criticism, Vol. I: A Checklist of Interpretation Since 1940 of English and American Plays* (Denver, Colorado: Alan Swallow, 1966), p. 41 [Secondary selected].

Halpern, Susan. "Bibliography," *Austin Clarke: His Life and Works* (Dublin: The Dolmen Press; New York: Humanities Press, 1974), pp. 188-195 [Primary. Secondary selected].

Kersnowski, Frank L., C. W. Spinks, and Laird Loomis. *A Bibliography of Modern Irish and Anglo-Irish Literature* (San Antonio, Texas: Trinity University Press, 1976), pp. 14-15 [Primary and secondary books].

Lyne, Gerard. "Austin Clarke: A Bibliography," *Irish University Review*, IV, No. 1 (Spring 1974), pp. 137-155 [Primary and secondary].

MacManus, M. J. "Bibliographies of Irish Writers, No. 8: Austin Clarke," *The Dublin Magazine*, X (April-June 1935), pp. 41-43 [Primary books].

Mac Namara, Brinsley, ed. *Abbey Plays 1899-1948* (Dublin: At the Sign of the Three Candles, [1949]) [Productions at the Abbey Theatre].

Mellown, Elgin W. *A Descriptive Catalogue of the Bibliographies of 20th Century British Poets, Novelists, and Dramatists* (Troy, New York: Whitston Publishing Company, 1978), pp. 63-64 [Primary and secondary bibliographies].

Miller, Liam. "The Books of Austin Clarke; A Checklist," *A Tribute to Austin Clarke on His Seventieth Birthday*, ed. John Montague and Liam Miller (Dublin: The Dolmen Press, 1966), pp. 23-27 [Primary books].

Temple, Ruth Z., and Martin Tucker. *Twentieth Century British Literature: A Reference Guide and Bibliography* (New York: Frederick Ungar, 1968), p. 147 [Primary books].

Willison, I. R., ed. *The New Cambridge Bibliography of English Literature, Vol. 4: 1900-1950* (Cambridge: Cambridge University Press, 1972), columns 248-249 [Primary books. Secondary selected].

COFFEY, Thomas (1925-   )

Hogan, Robert. "The Modern Drama," *Anglo-Irish Literature: A Review of Research*, ed. Richard J. Finneran (New York: Modern Language Association, 1976), p. 551 [Primary].

COLLIS, Robert (1900-1975)

Hogan, Robert. *After the Irish Renaissance; A Critical History of the Irish Drama Since 'The Plough and the Stars'* (Minneapolis: University of Minnesota Press, 1967; London: Macmillan, 1968), p. 262 [Primary books]; pp. 122-123 [Criticism].

COLUM, Padraic (1881-1972)

Bowen, Zack. *Padraic Colum; A Biographical-Critical Introduction* (Carbondale: Southern Illinois University Press, 1970), pp. 155-157 [Primary books].

Breed, Paul F., and Florence M. Sniderman. *Dramatic Criticism Index; A Bibliography of Commentaries on Playwrights from Ibsen to the Avant-Garde* (Detroit, Michigan: Gale Research Company, 1972), pp. 176-177 [Secondary selected].

Coleman, Arthur, and Gary R. Tyler. *Drama Criticism, Vol. I: A Checklist of Interpretation Since 1940 of English and American Plays* (Denver, Colorado: Alan Swallow, 1966), p. 42 [Secondary selected].

Denson, Alan. "Padraic Colum: An Appreciation with a Checklist of His Publications," *The Dublin Magazine,* VI, i (1967), pp. 50-67; ii, pp. 83-85 [Primary].

Hogan, Robert. "The Modern Drama," *Anglo-Irish Literature: A Review of Research,* ed. Richard J. Finneran (New York: Modern Language Association, 1976), p. 541 [Primary. Secondary selected].

Kersnowski, Frank L., C. W. Spinks, and Laird Loomis. *A Bibliography of Modern Irish and Anglo-Irish Literature* (San Antonio, Texas: Trinity University Press, 1976), pp. 15-21 [Primary books].

Lauterbach, Edward S., and W. Eugene Davis. *The Transitional Age: British Literature 1880-1920* (Troy, New York: Whitston Publishing Company, 1973), pp. 117-118 [Primary books. Secondary selected].

Longaker, Mark, and Edwin C. Bolles. *Contemporary English Literature* (New York: Appleton-Century-Crofts, 1953), pp. 49-50 [Primary books].

Mac Namara, Brinsley, ed. *Abbey Plays 1899-1948* (Dublin: At the Sign of the Three Candles, [1949]) [Productions at the Abbey Theatre].

Mellown, Elgin W. *A Descriptive Catalogue of the Bibliographies of 20th Century British Poets, Novelists, and Dramatists* (Troy, New York: Whitston Publishing Company, 1978), p. 66 [Primary and secondary bibliographies].

Millett, Fred B. *Contemporary British Literature; A Critical Survey and 232 Author Bibliographies* (New York: Harcourt, Brace, 1950), pp. 175-177 [Primary books. Secondary selected].

Nicoll, Allardyce. *English Drama 1900-1930; The Beginnings of the Modern Period* (Cambridge: Cambridge University Press, 1973), pp. 570-571 [First productions].

Samples, Gordon. *The Drama Scholars' Index to Plays and Filmscripts; A Guide to Plays and Filmscripts in Selected Anthologies, Series and Periodicals* (Metuchen, New Jersey: Scarecrow Press, 1974), p. 77 [Primary selected].

Temple, Ruth Z., and Martin Tucker. *Twentieth Century British Literature: A Reference Guide and Bibliography* (New York: Frederick Ungar, 1968), pp. 147-148 [Primary books].

Watson, George, ed. *The New Cambridge Bibliography of English Literature, Vol. 3: 1800-1900* (Cambridge: Cambridge University Press, 1969), columns 1942-1943 [Primary books. Secondary selected].

CONNELL, Norreys. See O'RIORDAN, Conal

CORKERY, Daniel (1878-1964)

Hogan, Robert. "The Modern Drama," *Anglo-Irish Literature: A Review of Research,* ed. Richard J. Finneran (New York: Modern Language Association, 1976), p. 540 [Primary. Secondary selected].

Kersnowski, Frank L., C. W. Spinks, and Laird Loomis. *A Bibliography of Modern Irish and Anglo-Irish Literature* (San Antonio, Texas: Trinity University Press, 1976), pp. 21-22 [Primary and secondary books].

Mac Namara, Brinsley, ed. *Abbey Plays 1899-1948* (Dublin: At the Sign of the Three Candles, [1949]) [Productions at the Abbey Theatre] .

Mellown, Elgin W. *A Descriptive Catalogue of the Bibliographies of 20th Century British Poets, Novelists, and Dramatists* (Troy, New York: Whitston Publishing Company, 1978), p. 73 [Primary and secondary bibliographies] .

Millett, Fred B. *Contemporary British Literature; A Critical Survey and 232 Author Bibliographies* (New York: Harcourt, Brace, 1935), pp. 185-186 [Primary books. Secondary selected] .

Nicoll, Allardyce. *English Drama 1900-1930; The Beginnings of the Modern Period* (Cambridge: Cambridge University Press, 1973), p. 576 [First productions] .

Samples, Gordon. *The Drama Scholars' Index to Plays and Filmscripts; A Guide to Plays and Filmscripts in Selected Anthologies, Series and Periodicals* (Metuchen, New Jersey: Scarecrow Press, 1974), p. 81 [Primary selected] .

Saul, G. B. "Bibliography," *Daniel Corkery. Irish Writers Series* (Lewisburg, Pennsylvania: Bucknell Univeristy Press, 1973), pp. 66-69 [Primary books. Secondary selected] .

Willison, I. R., ed. *The New Cambridge Bibliography of English Literature, Vol. 4: 1900-1950* (Cambridge: Cambridge University Press, 1972), columns 923-924 [Primary books. Secondary selected] .

§

COULTER, John (1888-   )

Hogan, Robert. "The Modern Drama," *Anglo-Irish Literature: A Review of Research,* ed. Richard J. Finneran (New York: Modern Language Association, 1976), p.

543 [Primary books].

Mac Namara, Brinsley, ed. *Abbey Plays 1899-1948* (Dublin: At the Sign of the Three Candles, [1949]) [Productions at the Abbey Theatre].

COUSINS, James [Sometimes as Seumas O'Cuisin] (1873-1956)

Denson, Alan. "Bio-Bibliographical Survey," *James H. Cousins and Margaret E. Cousins; A Bio-Bibliographical Survey* (Kendal: Alan Denson, 1967) [Primary and secondary].

Hogan, Robert. "The Modern Drama," *Anglo-Irish Literature: A Review of Research,* ed. Richard J. Finneran (New York: Modern Language Association, 1976), p. 537 [Primary. Secondary selected].

Mac Namara, Brinsley, ed. *Abbey Plays 1899-1948* (Dublin: At the Sign of the Three Candles, [1949]) [Productions at the Abbey Theatre].

D'ALTON, Louis (1900-1951)

Hogan, Robert. *After the Irish Renaissance; A Critical History of the Irish Drama Since 'The Plough and the Stars'* (Minneapolis: University of Minnesota Press, 1967; London: Macmillan, 1968), p. 262 [Primary books]; pp. 45-51 [Criticism].

Mac Namara, Brinsley, ed. *Abbey Plays 1899-1948* (Dublin: At the Sign of the Three Candles, [1949]) [Productions at the Abbey Theatre].

DE BURCA, Seamus [James A. Bourke] (1912-   )

Hogan, Robert. *After the Irish Renaissance; A Critical History of the Irish Drama Since 'The Plough and the Stars'* (Minneapolis: University of Minnesota Press, 1967; London: Macmillan, 1968), p. 262 [Primary books]; pp. 221-224 [Criticism].

DEEVY, Teresa (1894-1963)

Coleman, Arthur, and Gary R. Tyler. *Drama Criticism, Vol. I: A Checklist of Interpretation Since 1940 of English and American Plays* (Denver, Colorado: Alan Swallow, 1966), p. 48 [Secondary selected].

Hogan, Robert. *After the Irish Renaissance; A Critical History of the Irish Drama Since 'The Plough and the Stars'* (Minneapolis: University of Minnesota Press, 1967; London: Macmillan, 1968), p. 263 [Primary]; pp. 39-43 [Criticism].

Mac Namara, Brinsley, ed. *Abbey Plays 1899-1948* (Dublin: At the Sign of the Three Candles, [1949]) [Productions at the Abbey Theatre].

Mellown, Elgin W. *A Descriptive Catalogue of the Bibliographies of 20th Century British Poets, Novelists, and Dramatists* (Troy, New York: Whitston Publishing Company, 1978), p. 82 [Primary and secondary bibliographies].

Sahal, N. *Sixty Years of Realistic Irish Drama (1900-1960)* (Bombay: Macmillan, 1971), chap. 9 [Primary and criticism].

Samples, Gordon. *The Drama Scholars' Index to Plays and Filmscripts; A Guide to Plays and Filmscripts in Selected Anthologies, Series and Periodicals* (Metuchen, New Jersey: Scarecrow Press, 1974), p. 94 [Primary selected].

Willison, I. R., ed. *The New Cambridge Bibliography of English Literature, Vol. 4: 1900-1950* (Cambridge: Cambridge University Press, 1972), columns 931-932 [Primary. Secondary selected].

DONLEAVY, J[ames] P[atrick] (1926-   )

Elsom, John. "J. P. Donleavy," *Contemporary Dramatists,* ed. James Vinson (London: St. James Press; New York: St. Martin's Press, 1973), pp. 204-205 [Primary books]; pp. 205-206 [Criticism].

Hogan, Robert. *After the Irish Renaissance; A Critical History of the Irish Drama Since 'The Plough and the Stars'* (Minneapolis: University of Minnesota Press, 1967; London: Macmillan, 1968), p. 263 [Primary books]; pp. 230-231 [Criticism].

DOUGLAS, James (1929-   )

Hogan, Robert. *After the Irish Renaissance; A Critican History of the Irish Drama Since 'The Plough and the Stars'* (Minneapolis: University of Minnesota Press, 1967; London: Macmillan, 1968), p. 263 [Primary]; pp. 192-195 [Criticism].

—. "The Modern Drama," *Anglo-Irish Literature: A Review of Research,* ed. Richard J. Finneran (New York: Modern Language Association, 1976), p. 552 [Primary].

British and Continental Drama from Ibsen to Pinter (Metuchen, New Jersey: Scarecrow Press, 1968), pp. 89-90 [Secondary selected].

Samples, Gordon. *The Drama Scholars' Index to Plays and Filmscripts; A Guide to Plays and Filmscripts in Selected Anthologies, Series and Periodicals* (Metuchen, New Jersey: Scarecrow Press, 1974), p. 109 [Primary selected].

Stoddard, F. G. "The Lord Dunsany Collection," *Library Chronicle of the University of Texas,* IX, No. 3 (1967), 2732 [Discussive essay with particular attention to MSS at Texas].

Temple, Ruth Z., and Martin Tucker. *Twentieth Century British Literature: A Reference Guide and Bibliography* (New York: Frederick Ungar, 1968), p. 158 [Primary books. Secondary selected].

Watson, George, ed. *The New Cambridge Bibliography of English Literature, Vol. 3: 1800-1900* (Cambridge: Cambridge University Press, 1969), columns 1945-1948 [Primary books. Secondary selected].

ERVINE, St. John Greer (1883-1971)

Adelman, Irving, and Rita Dworkin. *Modern Drama; A Checklist of Critical Literature on 20th Century Plays* (Metuchen, New Jersey: Scarecrow Press, 1967), p. 104 [Secondary selected].

Batho, Edith Clara, and Bonamy Dobrée. *The Victorians and After, 1830-1914.* Introduction to English Literature, Vol. iv. General Editor Bonamy Dobrée (London: Cresset Press; New York: R. M. McBride, 1938), p. 272 [Primary books].

Breed, Paul F., and Florence M. Sniderman. *Dramatic Criticism Index; A Bibliography of Commentaries on Play-*

wrights from Ibsen to the Avant-Garde (Detroit, Michigan: Gale Research Company, 1972), pp. 215-216 [Secondary selected].

Howard, Paula. "St. John Ervine: A Bibliography of His Published Work," *Irish Booklore* (1971), pp. 203-209 [Primary].

Kersnowski, Frank L., C. W. Spinks, and Laird Loomis. *A Bibliography of Modern Irish and Anglo-Irish Literature* (San Antonio, Texas: Trinity University Press, 1976), pp. 38-42 [Primary books].

Lauterbach, Edward S., and W. Eugene Davis. *The Transitional Age: British Literature 1880-1920* (Troy, New York: Whitston Publishing Company, 1973), pp. 144-145 [Primary books. Secondary selected].

Longaker, Mark, and Edwin C. Bolles. *Contemporary English Literature* (New York: Appleton-Century-Crofts, 1953), p. 63 [Primary books].

Mac Namara, Brinsley, ed. *Abbey Plays 1899-1948* (Dublin: At the Sign of the Three Candles, [1949]) [Productions at the Abbey Theatre].

Mellown, Elgin W. *A Descriptive Catalogue of the Bibliographies of 20th Century British Poets, Novelists, and Dramatists* (Troy, New York: Whitston Publishing Company, 1978), p. 106 [Secondary bibliographies].

Millett, Fred B. *Contemporary British Literature; A Critical Survey and 232 Author Bibliographies* (New York: Harcourt, Brace, 1935), pp. 220-222 [Primary books. Secondary selected].

Nicoll, Allardyce. *English Drama 1900-1930; The Beginnings of the Modern Period* (Cambridge: Cambridge University Press, 1973), pp. 632-633 [First productions].

Salem, James M. *A Guide to Critical Reviews. Part III: British and Continental Drama from Ibsen to Pinter* (Metuchen, New Jersey: Scarecrow Press, 1968), pp. 93-

95 [Secondary selected] .

Samples, Gordon. *The Drama Scholars' Index to Plays and Filmscripts; A Guide to Plays and Filmscripts in Selected Anthologies, Series and Periodicals* (Metuchen, New Jersey: Scarecrow Press, 1974), p. 117 [Primary selected] .

Temple, Ruth Z., and Martin Tucker. *Twentieth Century British Literature: A Reference Guide and Bibliography* (New York: Frederick Ungar, 1968), p. 160 [Primary books] .

Watson, George, ed. *The New Cambridge Bibliography of English Literature, Vol. 3: 1800-1900* (Cambridge: Cambridge University Press, 1969), column 1945 [Primary books. Secondary selected] .

FALLON, Padraic (1906-1974)

Hogan, Robert. *After the Irish Renaissance; A Critical History of the Irish Drama Since 'The Plough and the Stars'* (Minneapolis: University of Minnesota Press, 1967; London: Macmillan, 1968), pp. 159-163, 264 [Criticism] .

—. "The Modern Drama," *Anglo-Irish Literature: A Review of Research,* ed. Richard J. Finneran (New York: Modern Language Association, 1976), pp. 546-548 [Primary. Secondary selected] .

Mellown, Elgin W. *A Descriptive Catalogue of the Bibliographies of 20th Century British Poets, Novelists, and Dramatists* (Troy, New York: Whitston Publishing Company, 1978), p. 108 [Primary and secondary bibliographies] .

FARRINGTON, Conor (1928-   )

Hogan, Robert. *After the Irish Renaissance; A Critical History of the Irish Drama Since 'The Plough and the Stars'* (Minneapolis: University of Minnesota Press, 1967; London: Macmillan, 1968), p. 264 [Primary] ; pp. 158-159 [Criticism] .

FITZMAURICE, George (1877-1963)

Breed, Paul, F., and Florence M. Sniderman. *Dramatic Criticism Index; A Bibliography of Commentaries on Playwrights from Isben to the Avant-Garde* (Detroit, Michigan: Gale Research Company, 1972), pp. 220-221 [Secondary selected] .

Coleman, Arthur, and Gary R. Tyler. *Drama Criticism, Vol. I: A Checklist of Interpretation Since 1940 of English and American Plays* (Denver, Colorado: Alan Swallow, 1966), p. 71 [Secondary selected] .

Henderson, Joanne L.   "Checklist," *Journal of Irish Literature*, I, No. 2 (May 1972), pp. 101-104 [Primary. Secondary selected] .

Hogan, Robert.   "The Modern Drama," *Anglo-Irish Literature: A Review of Research*, ed. Richard J. Finneran (New York: Modern Language Association, 1976), p. 538 [Primary. Secondary selected] .

Kersnowski, Frank L., C. W. Spinks, and Laird Loomis. *A Bibliography of Modern Irish and Anglo-Irish Literature* (San Antonio, Texas: Trinity University Press, 1976), p. 42 [Primary and secondary books] .

Mac Namara, Brinsley, ed. *Abbey Plays 1899-1948* (Dublin: At the Sign of the Three Candles, [1949]) [Productions at the Abbey Theatre] .

Mellown, Elgin W. *A Descriptive Catalogue of the Bibliographies of 20th Century British Poets, Novelists, and Dramatists* (Troy, New York: Whitston Publishing Company, 1978), pp. 112-113 [Primary and secondary bibliographies].

Miller, Liam. "George Fitzmaurice: A Bibliographical Note," *Irish Writing* (Cork), No. 15 (June 1951), pp. 47-48 [Primary. First productions].

Nicoll, Allardyce. *English Drama 1900-1930; The Beginnings of the Modern Period* (Cambridge: Cambridge University Press, 1973), pp. 646-647 [First productions].

The Plays of George Fitzmaurice, 3 vols. (Dublin: Dolmen Press, 1967-70) [The three Introductions provide references to the secondary bibliography].

Slaughter, Howard K. *George Fitzmaurice and His Enchanted Land* (Dublin: The Dolmen Press, 1972), pp. 55-56 [Abbey Theatre productions of the plays]; pp. 57-59 [Primary].

Watson, George, ed. *The New Cambridge Bibliography of English Literature, Vol. 3: 1800-1900* (Cambridge: Cambridge University Press, 1969), columns 1941-1942 [Primary books. Secondary selected].

FORBES, Dick (-   )

Hogan, Robert. *After the Irish Renaissance; A Critical History of the Irish Drama after 'The Plough and the Stars'* (Minneapolis: University of Minnesota Press, 1967; London: Macmillan, 1968), p. 264 [Primary books].

FRIEL, Brian (1929-   )

Bigsby, C. W. E. "Brian Friel," *Contemporary Dramatists,*
ed. James Vinson (London: St. James Press; New York:
St. Martin's Press, 1973), pp. 267-268 [Primary books] ;
pp. 268-269 [Criticism] .

Hogan, Robert. *After the Irish Renaissance; A Critical History of the Irish Drama Since 'The Plough and the Stars'*
(Minneapolis: University of Minnesota Press, 1967; London: Macmillan, 1968), p. 264 [Primary books] ; pp.
195-197 [Criticism] .

—. "The Modern Drama," *Anglo-Irish Literature: A Review
of Research,* ed. Richard J. Finneran (New York: Modern
Language Association, 1976), p. 552 [Primary. Secondary selected] .

Maxwell, D. E. S. *Brian Friel.*   The Irish Writers series
(Lewisburg, Pennsylvania: Bucknell University Press,
1973), pp. 111-112 [Primary books. Secondary select-
ed] .

Mellown, Elgin W. *A Descriptive Catalogue of the Bibliographies of 20th Century British Poets, Novelists, and
Dramatists* (Troy, New York: Whitston Publishing Company, 1978), pp. 121-122 [Primary and secondary bib-
liographies] .

Salem, James M. *A Guide to Critical Reviews, Part III:
British and Continental Drama from Ibsen to Pinter*
(Metuchen, New Jersey: Scarecrow Press, 1968), pp. 97-
98 [Secondary periodicals] .

Samples, Gordon. *The Drama Scholars' Index to Plays and
Filmscripts; A Guide to Plays and Filmscripts in Selected
Anthologies, Series and Periodicals* (Metuchen, New Jer-
sey: Scarecrow Press, 1974), p. 136 [Primary selected] .

GALLIVAN, G. P. (1920-   )

Hogan, Robert. *After the Irish Renaissance; A Critical History of the Irish Drama Since 'The Plough and the Stars'* (Minneapolis: University of Minnesota Press, 1967; London: Macmillan, 1968), p. 264 [Primary books] ; pp. 189-192 [Criticism] .

GOGARTY, Oliver St. John (1878-1957)

Carens, James F.   "Oliver St. John Gogarty," *Anglo-Irish Literature; A Review of Research,* ed. Richard J. Finneran (New York: Modern Language Association, 1976), pp. 452-459 [Secondary annotated] .

Hewson, Michael.   "Gogarty's Authorship of *Blight,*" *Irish Book,* I (Spring 1959), pp. 19-20 [Primary] .

Kersnowski, Frank L., C. W. Spinks, and Laird Loomis. *A Bibliography of Modern Irish and Anglo-Irish Literature* (San Antonio, Texas: Trinity University Press, 1976), pp. 43-45 [Primary and secondary books] .

Longaker, Mark, and Edwin C. Bolles. *Contemporary English Literature* (New York: Appleton-Century-Crofts, 1953), p. 488 [Primary books] .

Mac Namara, Brinsley, ed. *Abbey Plays 1899-1948* (Dublin: At the Sign of the Three Candles, [1949]) [Productions of plays at the Abbey Theatre] .

Mellown, Elgin W.   *A Descriptive Catalogue of the Bibliographies of 20th Century British Poets, Novelists, and Dramatists* (Troy, New York: Whitston Publishing Company, 1978), p. 133 [Primary and secondary bibliographies] .

Nicoll, Allardyce. *English Drama 1900-1930; The Beginnings of the Modern Period* (Cambridge: Cambridge University

Press, 1973), p. 471 [First productions].

O'Connor, Ulick. *The Times I've Seen: Oliver St. John Gogarty; A Biography* (New York: Ivan Obolensky, 1963), pp. 351-357. British edition entitled *Oliver St. John Gogarty; A Poet and His Times* (London: Jonathan Cape, 1964), pp. 305-310 [General bibliography. Other bibliographical information in text, *passim*].

Temple, Ruth Z., and Martin Tucker. *Twentieth Century British Literature: A Reference Guide the Bibliography* (New York: Frederick Ungar, 1968), p. 168 [Primary books].

Willison, I. R., ed. *The New Cambridge Bibliography of English Literature, Vol. 4: 1900-1950* (Cambridge: Cambridge University Press, 1972), columns 283-284 [Primary books. Secondary selected].

GREGORY, Lady Isabella Augusta (1859-1932)

Adelman, Irving, and Rita Dworkin. *Modern Drama; A Checklist of Critical Literature on 20th Century Plays* (Metuchen: New Jersey: Scarecrow Press, 1967), pp. 132-133 [Secondary selected].

Batho, Edith Clara, and Bonamy Dobrée. *The Victorians and After, 1830-1914.* Introductions to English Literature, Vol. IV. General Editor Bonamy Dobrée (London: Cresset Press; New York: R. M. McBride, 1938), p. 271 [Primary books].

Breed, Paul F., and Florence M. Sniderman. *Dramatic Criticism Index; A Bibliography of Commentaries on Playwrights from Ibsen to the Avant-Garde* (Detroit, Michigan: Gale Research Company, 1972), pp. 281-283 [Secondary selected].

Carens, James F. "Lady Gregory," *Anglo-Irish Literature; A*

Review of Research, ed. Richard J. Finneran (New York: Modern Language Association, 1976), pp. 437-446 [Secondary annotated] .

Coleman, Arthur, and Gary R. Tyler. *Drama Criticism, Vol. I: A Checklist of Interpretation Since 1940 of English and American Plays* (Denver, Colorado: Alan Swallow, 1966), p. 87 [Secondary selected] .

Coxhead, Elizabeth. *John Millington Synge and Lady Gregory* (London: Longmans, Green, 1962), pp. 34-35 [Primary books.] .

—. *Lady Gregory; A Literary Portrait.* Second Edition Revised and Enlarged (London: Secker & Warburg, 1966), pp. 219-220 ["Lady Gregory's Principal Publications"] .

Kersnowski, Frank L., C. W. Spinks, and Laird Loomis. *A Bibliography of Modern Irish and Anglo-Irish Literature* (San Antonio, Texas: Trinity University Press, 1976), pp. 48-53 [Primary and secondary books] .

Klenze, Hilda V. *Lady Gregorys Leben und Werk* (Bochum-Langendreer: Heinrich Pöppinghaus O. H.-G., 1940; New York: Johnson Reprint, 1966), pp. 90-91 [Primary books] .

Lauterbach, Edward S., and W. Eugene Davis. *The Transitional Age: British Literature 1880-1920* (Troy, New York: Whitston Publishing Company, 1973), pp. 163-164 [Primary books. Secondary selected] .

Longaker, Mark, and Edwin C. Bolles. *Contemporary English Literature* (New York: Appleton-Century-Crofts, 1953), pp. 57-59 [Primary books. Secondary selected] .

Mellown, Elgin W. *A Descriptive Catalogue of the Bibliographies of 20th Century British Poets, Novelists, and Dramatists* (Troy, New York: Whitston Publishing Company, 1978), pp. 146-147 [Primary and secondary bibliographies] .

Mikhail, E. H. "The Theatre of Lady Gregory," *Bulletin of*

Bibliography, XXVII, No. 1 (January-March 1970), pp. 9-10 [Secondary].

Millett, Fred B. *Contemporary British Literature; A Critical Survey and 232 Author Bibliographies* (New York: Harcourt, Brace, 1935), pp. 257-259 [Primary books. Secondary selected].

Nicoll, Allardyce. *English Drama 1900-1930; The Beginnings of the Modern Period* (Cambridge: Cambridge University Press, 1973), pp. 685-687 [First productions].

Salem, James M. *A Guide to Critical Reviews. Part III: British and Continental Drama from Ibsen to Pinter* (Metuchen, New Jersey: Scarecrow Press, 1968), pp. 115-116 [Secondary selected].

Samples, Gordon. *The Drama Scholars' Index to Plays and Filmscripts; A Guide to Plays and Filmscripts in Selected Anthologies, Series and Periodicals* (Metuchen, New Jersey: Scarecrow Press, 1974), p. 157 [Primary selected].

Temple, Ruth Z., and Martin Tucker. *Twentieth Century British Literature: A Reference Guide and Bibliography* (New York: Frederick Ungar, 1968), p. 172 [Primary books. Secondary selected].

Watson, George, ed. *The New Cambridge Bibliography of English Literature, Vol. 3: 1800-1900* (Cambridge: Cambridge University Press, 1969), columns 1939-1941 [Primary books. Secondary selected].

HEALY, Gerard (1918-1963)

Hogan, Robert. *After the Irish Renaissance; A Critical History of the Irish Drama Since 'The Plough and the Stars'* (Minneapolis: University of Minnesota Press, 1967; London: Macmillan, 1968), p. 265 [Primary books]; pp. 224-226 [Criticism].

Mac Namara, Brinsley, ed. *Abbey Plays 1899-1948* (Dublin: At the Sign of the Three Candles, [1949]) [Productions at the Abbey Theatre].

HEPPENSTALL, W. D. (-   )

Hogan, Robert. *After the Irish Renaissance; A Critical History of the Irish Drama Since 'The Plough and the Stars'* (Minneapolis: University of Minnesota Press, 1967; London: Macmillan, 1968), p. 265 [Primary books].

Mellown, Elgin W. *A Descriptive Catalogue of the Bibliographies of 20th Century British Poets, Novelists, and Dramatists* (Troy, New York: Whitston Publishing Company, 1978), p. 160 [Primary and secondary bibliographies].

HIGGINS, F[rederick] R[obert] (1896-1941)

Hogan, Robert. "The Modern Drama," *Anglo-Irish Literature: A Review of Research*, ed. Richard J. Finneran (New York: Modern Language Association, 1976), pp. 543-544 [Primary. Secondary selected].

MacManus, M. J. "Bibliography of F. R. Higgins," *The Dublin Magazine*, XXI (July-September 1946), pp. 43-45 [Primary books].

Mac Namara, Brinsley, ed. *Abbey Plays 1899-1948* (Dublin: At the Sign of the Three Candles, [1949]) [Productions at the Abbey Theatre].

Mellown, Elgin W. *A Descriptive Catalogue of the Bibliographies of 20th Century British Poets, Novelists, and Dramatists* (Troy, New York: Whitston Publishing Company, 1978), p. 163 [Primary and secondary bibliographies] .

Willison, I. R., ed. *The New Cambridge Bibliography of English Literature, Vol. 4: 1900-1950* (Cambridge: Cambridge University Press, 1972), column 290 [Primary books. Secondary selected] .

HYDE, Douglas (1860-1949)

Breed, Paul F., and Florence M. Sniderman. *Dramatic Index; A Bibliography of Commentaries on Playwrights from Ibsen to the Avant-Garde* (Detroit, Michigan: Gale Research Company, 1972), p. 314 [Secondary books] .

Hogan, Robert. "The Modern Drama," *Anglo-Irish Literature: A Review of Research*, ed. Richard J. Finneran (New York: Modern Language Association, 1976), pp. 533-534 [Primary books. Secondary selected] .

Kersnowski, Frank L., C. W. Spinks, and Laird Loomis. *A Bibliography of Modern Irish and Anglo-Irish Literature* (San Antonio, Texas: Trinity University Press, 1976), pp. 54-60 [Primary and secondary books] .

Mac Namara, Brinsley, ed. *Abbey Plays 1899-1948* (Dublin: At the Sing of the Three Candles, [1949]) [Productions at the Abbey Theatre] .

Mellown, Elgin W. *A Descriptive Catalogue of the Bibliographies of 20th Century British Poets, Novelists, and Dramatists* (Troy, New York: Whitston Publishing Company, 1978), p. 181 [Primary and secondary bibliographies] .

Millett, Fred B. *Contemporary British Literature; A Critical Survey and 232 Author Bibliographies* (New York: Harcourt, Brace, 1935), pp. 290-292 [Primary books. Secondary selected] .

Nicoll, Allardyce. *English Drama 1900-1930; The Beginnings of the Modern Period* (Cambridge: Cambridge University Press, 1973), p. 744 [First productions].

O'Hegarty, Patrick Sarsfield. "A Bibliography of Dr. Douglas Hyde," *The Dublin Magazine,* XIV (January-March 1939), pp. 57-66; XIV (April-June 1939), pp. 72-78. Reprinted as pamphlet, *A Bibliography of Dr. Douglas Hyde* (Dublin: Privately printed, 1939) [Primary books].

Watson, George, ed. *The New Cambridge Bibliography of English Literature, Vol. 3: 1800-1900* (Cambridge: Cambridge University Press, 1969), columns 1909-1910 [Primary books. Secondary selected].

JOHNSTON, [William] Denis (1901-   )

Breed, Paul F., and Florence M. Sniderman. *Dramatic Criticism Index; A Bibliography of Commentaries on Playwrights from Ibsen to the Avant-Garde* (Detroit, Michigan: Gale Research Company, 1972), pp. 357-358 [Secondary selected].

Daiches, David. *The Present Age, After 1920.* Introductions to English Literature, Vol. V. General Editor Bonamy Dobrée (London: Cresset Press; Bloomington, Indiana: Indiana University Press, 1958), p. 329 [Primary books].

Ferrar, Harold. *Denis Johnston's Irish Theatre* (Dublin: The Dolmen Press; New York: Humanities Press, 1973), pp. 143-144 [Primary. Secondary selected].

Kersnowski, Frank L., C. W. Spinks, and Laird Loomis. *A Bibliography of Modern Irish and Anglo-Irish Literature* (San Antonio, Texas: Trinity University Press, 1976), pp. 60-61 [Primary and secondary books].

Mac Namara, Brinsley, ed. *Abbey Plays 1899-1948* (Dublin: At the Sign of the Three Candles [1949]) [Productions at the Abbey Theatre] .

Mellown, Elgin W. *A Descriptive Catalogue of the Bibli-ographies of 20th Century British Poets, Novelists, and Dramatists* (Troy, New York: Whitston Publishing Company, 1978), p. 187 [Primary and secondary bibliographies] .

Salem, James M. *A Guide to Critical Reviews. Part III: British and Continental Drama from Ibsen to Pinter* (Metuchen, New Jersey: Scarecrow Press, 1968), p. 141 [Secondary selected] .

Spinner, Kaspar. *Die Alte Dame Sagt: Nein! Irische Dramatiker. Lennox Robinson, Sean O'Casey, Denis Johnston.* Schweizer Anglistische Arbeiten 52 (Bern: Francke Verlag, 1961), pp. 208-209 [Primary selected] , pp. 209-210 [Secondary selected] .

Strachan, Alan. "Denis Johnston," *Contemporary Dramatists,* ed. James Vinson (London: St. James Press; New York: St. Martin's Press, 1973), pp. 415-417 [Primary books] ; pp. 417-419 [Criticism] .

Temple, Ruth Z., and Martin Tucker. *Twentieth Century British Literature: A Reference Guide and Bibliography* (New York: Frederick Ungar, 1968), p. 185 [Primary books] .

Willison, I. R., ed. *The New Cambridge Bibliography of English Literature, Vol. 4: 1900-1950* (Cambridge: Cambridge University Press, 1972), columns 957-958 [Primary. Secondary selected] .

JOYCE, James (1882-1941)

Adelman, Irving, and Rita Dworkin. *Modern Drama; A Checklist of Critical Literature on 20th Century Plays* (Metuchen, New Jersey: Scarecrow Press, 1967), pp. 174-

176 [Secondary selected] .

Beebe, Maurice, Phillip F. Herring, and Walton Litz. "Criticism of James Joyce: A Selected Checklist," *Modern Fiction Studies,* XV (Spring 1969), pp. 105-182 [Primary and secondary selected] .

Breed, Paul F., and Florence M. Sniderman. *Dramatic Criticism Index; A Bibliography of Commentaries on Playwrights from Ibsen to Avant-Garde* (Detroit, Michigan: Gale Research Company, 1972), p. 361 [Secondary selected] .

Cohn, Alan M. *James Joyce: An Exhibition from the Collection of Dr. H. K. Croessmann* (Carbondale, Illinois: Southern Illinois University Press, 1957) [At Southern Illinois University] .

—, and Richard M. Kain. "Supplemental James Joyce Checklist, 1962," *James Joyce Quarterly,* I (Winter 1964), pp. 15-22 [Primary and secondary]. Continued by Cohn and others in subsequent issues.

—. "Joyce Bibliographies: A Survey," *American Book Collector,* XV (Summer 1965), pp. 11-16 [Primary and secondary bibliographies] .

Coleman, Arthur, and Gary R. Tyler. *Drama Criticism, Vol. I: A Checklist of Interpretation Since 1940 of English and American Plays* (Denver, Colorado: Alan Swallow, 1966), pp. 110 [Secondary selected] .

Daiches, David. *The Present Age After 1920* (London: The Cresset Press, 1958), pp. 265-266 [Primary books. Secondary selected] .

Deming, Robert H. *A Bibliography of James Joyce Studies* (Lawrence: University of Kansas Libraries, 1964) [Primary and secondary bibliographies] .

James Joyce Quarterly, 1962 to the present. Includes a continuing "Supplemental JJ checklist" [Secondary] .

Kersnowski, Frank L., C. W. Spinks, and Laird Loomis. *A Bibliography of Modern Irish and Anglo-Irish Literature* (San Antonio, Texas: Trinity University Press, 1976), pp. 61-64 [Primary and secondary books].

Longaker, Mark, and Edwin C. Bolles. *Contemporary English Literature* (New York: Appleton-Century-Crofts, 1953), pp. 350-356 [Primary books. Secondary selected].

McCoy, Ralph E. "Manuscript Collections in Morris Library," *1 Carb S*, I, No. 2 (Spring-Summer 1974), pp. 153-162.

Mellown, Elgin W. *A Descriptive Catalogue of the Bibliographies of 20th Century British Poets, Novelists, and Dramatists* (Troy, New York: Whitston Publishing Company, 1978), pp. 189-191 [Primary and secondary bibliographies].

Millett, Fred B. *Contemporary British Literature; A Critical Survey and 232 Author Bibliographies* (New York: Harcourt, Brace, 1935), pp. 301-303 [Primary books. Secondary selected].

Nicoll, Allardyce. *English Drama 1900-1930; The Beginnings of the Modern Period* (Cambridge: Cambridge University Press, 1973), p. 759 [First productions].

O'Hegarty, P. S. "Bibliography of James Joyce," *The Dublin Magazine*, XXI, No. 1 (January-March 1946), pp. 38-47 [Primary books].

Palmer, Helen H., and Anne Jane Dyson. *European Drama Criticism* (Hamden, Connecticut: Shoe String Press, 1968), p. 233; *Supplement I* (1970), p. 105; *Supplement II*, (1974), pp. 88-90 [Secondary selected].

Parker, Alan. *James Joyce: A Bibliography of His Writings, Critical Material and Miscellanea* (Bouston: F. W. Faxon, 1948).

Salem, James M. *A Guide to Critical Reviews, Part III: British and Continential Drama from Ibsen to Pinter*

(Metuchen, New Jersey: Scarecrow, 1968), p. 144 [Secondary periodicals].

Samples, Gordon. *The Drama Scholars' Index to Plays and Filmscripts; A Guide to Plays and Filmscripts in Selected Anthologies, Series and Periodicals* (Metuchen, New Jersey: Scarecrow Press, 1974), p. 202 [Primary selected].

Scholes, Robert. *The Cornell Joyce Collection: A Catalogue* (Ithaca: Cornell University Press, 1961) [At Cornell University].

Slocum, John J., and Herbert Cahoon. *A Bibliography of James Joyce, 1882-1941* (London: Rupert Hart-Davis; New Haven: Yale University, 1953) [Primary].

Spielberg, Peter. *James Joyce's Manuscripts and Letters at the University of Buffalo: A Catalogue* (Buffalo, New York: University of Buffalo, 1962).

Staley, Thomas F. "James Joyce," *Anglo-Irish Literature; A Review of Research,* ed. Richard J. Finneran (New York: Modern Language Association, 1976), pp. 366-435 [Secondary annotated].

Temple, Ruth Z., ane Martin Tucker. *Twentieth Century British Literature: A Reference Guide and Bibliography* (New York: Frederick Ungar, 1968), p. 186 [Primary books. Secondary selected].

W[hite], W[illiam]. "James Joyce," *The New Cambridge Bibliography of English Literature,* vol. IV, 1900-1950, ed. I. R. Willison (Cambridge: Cambridge University Press, 1972), columns 444-472 [Primary. Secondary selected].

KEANE, John B. (1928-   )

Henderson, Joanne L. "Checklist," *Journal of Irish Litera-*

ture, I, No. 2 (May 1972), pp. 118-119 [Primary].

Hogan, Robert. *After the Irish Renaissance; A Critical History of the Irish Drama Since 'The Plough and the Stars'* (Minneapolis: University of Minnesota Press, 1967; London: Macmillan, 1968), p. 265 [Primary books], pp. 208-220 [Criticism].

—. "The Modern Drama," *Anglo-Irish Literature: A Review of Research,* ed. Richard J. Finneran (New York: Modern Language Association, 1976), pp. 552-553 [Primary].

Kinsman, Clare D., and Mary Ann Tennenhouse, ed. *Contemporary Authors; A Bio-Bibliographical Guide to Current Authors and Their Works* (Detroit: Gale Research Company, 1972), pp. 318-319 [Primary books].

Mellown, Elgin W. *A Descriptive Catalogue of the Bibliographies of 20th Century British Poets, Novelists, and Dramatists* (Troy, New York: Whitston Publishing Company, 1978), p. 193 [Primary and secondary bibliographies].

KILROY, Thomas (1936-   )

Hogan, Robert. "The Modern Drama," *Anglo-Irish Literature: A Review of Research,* ed. Richard J. Finneran (New York: Modern Language Association, 1976), p. 552 [Primary].

LEONARD, Hugh [John Keyes Byrne] (1926-   )

Billington, Michael. "Hugh Leonard," *Contemporary Dramatists,* ed. James Vinson (London: St. James Press; New York: St. Martin's Press, 1973), pp. 468-469 [Primary books] pp. 469-471 [Criticism] .

Breed, Paul F., and Florence M. Sniderman. *Dramatic Criticism Index; A Bibliography of Commentaries on Playwrights from Ibsen to the Avant-Garde* (Detroit, Michigan: Gale Research Company, 1972), pp. 386-387 [Secondary selected] .

Hogan, Robert. *After the Irish Renaissance; A Critical History of the Irish Drama Since 'The Plough and the Stars'* (Minneapolis: University of Minnesota Press, 1967; London: Macmillan, 1968), p. 265 [Primary] ; pp. 186-189 [Criticism] .

—. "The Modern Drama," *Anglo-Irish Literature: A Review of Research*, ed. Richard J. Finneran (New York: Modern Language Association, 1976), p. 551 [Primary] .

Mellown, Elgin W. *A Descriptive Catalogue of the Bibliographies of 20th Century British Poets, Novelists, and Dramatists* (Troy, New York: Whitston Publishing Company, 1978), p. 209 [Primary and secondary bibliographies] .

Samples, Gordon. *The Drama Scholars' Index to Plays and Filmscripts; A Guide to Plays and Filmscripts in Selected Anthologies, Series and Periodicals* (Metuchen, New Jersey: Scarecrow Press, 1974), pp. 224-225 [Primary selected] .

LETTS, Winifred M. [Mrs. W. H. Verschoyle] (1882-   )

Longaker, Mark, and Edwin C. Bolles. *Contemporary English Literature* (New York: Appleton-Century-Crofts, 1953), pp. 50-51 [Primary books] .

Mac Namara, Brinsley, ed. *Abbey Plays 1899-1948* (Dublin: At the Sign of the Three Candles, [1949]) [Productions at the Abbey Theatre] .

Mellown, Elgin W. *A Descriptive Catalogue of the Bibliographies of 20th Century British Poets, Novelists, and Dramatists* (Troy, New York: Whitston Publishing Company, 1978), pp. 210-211 [Primary and secondary bibliographies] .

Nicoll, Allardyce. *English Drama 1900-1930; The Beginnings of the Modern Period* (Cambridge: Cambridge University Press, 1973), p. 783 [First productions] .

LONGFORD, Earl of [Edward Arthur Henry Pakenham]
(1902-1961)

Hogan, Robert. *After the Irish Renaissance; a Critical History of the Irish Drama Since 'The Plough and the Stars'* (Minneapolis: University of Minnesota Press, 1967; London: Macmillan, 1968), pp. 265-266 [Primary books] ; pp. 125-126 [Criticism] .

LONGFORD, Countess of [Nee Christine Patti Trew]
(1900-   )

Hogan, Robert. *After the Irish Renaissance; A Critical History of the Irish Drama Since 'The Plough and the Stars'* (Minneapolis: University of Minnesota Press, 1967; London: Macmillan, 1968), p. 266 [Primary books] ; pp. 126-132 [Criticism] .

Mac ARDLE, Dorothy (1889-   )

Mac Namara, Brinsley, ed. *Abbey Plays 1899-1948* (Dublin:

At the Sign of the Three Candles, [1949]) [Productions at the Abbey Theatre] .

Malone, Andrew E. *The Irish Drama* (London: Constable; New York: Scribner's 1929), p. 269 [Primary and criticism] .

Nicoll, Allardyce. *English Drama 1900-1930; The Beginnings of the Modern Period* (Cambridge: Cambridge University Press, 1973), p. 797 [First productions] .

McCANN, John (1905-   )

Hogan, Robert. *After the Irish Renaissance; A Critical History of the Irish Drama Since 'The Plough and the Stars'* (Minneapolis: University of Minnesota Press, 1967; London: Macmillan, 1968), p. 266 [Primary books] .

MacDONAGH, Donagh (1912-1968)

Breed, Paul F., and Florence M. Sniderman. *Dramatic Criticism Index; A Bibliography of Commentaries on Playwrights from Ibsen to the Avant-Garde* (Detroit, Michigan: Gale Research Company, 1972), p. 394 [Secondary selected] .

Hogan, Robert. *After the Irish Renaissance; A Critical History of the Irish Drama Since 'The Plough and the Stars'* (Minneapolis: University of Minnesota Press, 1967; London: Macmillan, 1968), p. 266 [Primary books] ; pp. 154-158 [Criticism] .

—. "The Modern Drama," *Anglo-Irish Literature: A Review of Research,* ed. Richard J. Finneran (New York: Modern Language Association, 1976), p. 549 [Primary] .

Kersnowski, Frank L., C. W. Spinks, and Laird Loomis. *A Bibliography of Modern Irish and Anglo-Irish Literature* (San Antonio, Texas: Trinity University Press, 1976), pp. 70-71 [Primary books].

Mellown, Elgin W. *A Descriptive Catalogue of the Bibliographies of 20th Century British Poets, Novelists, and Dramatists* (Troy, New York: Whitston Publishing Company, 1978), p. 223 [Primary and secondary bibliographies].

Willison, I. R., ed. *The New Cambridge Bibliography of English Literature, Vol. 4: 1900-1950* (Cambridge: Cambridge University Press, 1972), column 963 [Primary. Second selected].

MacDONAGH, Thomas (1878-1916)

Kersnowski, Frank L., C. W. Spinks, and Laird Loomis. *A Bibliography of Modern Irish and Anglo-Irish Literature* (San Antonio, Texas: Trinity University Press, 1976), pp. 71-72 [Primary and secondary books].

Mellown, Elgin W. *A Descriptive Catalogue of the Bibliographies of 20th Century British Poets, Novelists, and Dramatists* (Troy, New York: Whitston Publishing Company, 1978), p. 223 [Primary and secondary bibliographies].

Nicoll, Allardyce. *English Drama 1900-1930; The Beginnings of the Modern Period* (Cambridge: Cambridge University Press, 1973), p. 800 [First productions].

O'Hegarty, Patrick Sarsfield. "Bibliographies of 1916 and the Irish Revolution No. 2: Thomas MacDonagh," *The Dublin Magazine,* VII (January-March 1932), pp. 26-29 [Primary books].

Parks, Edd Winfield, and Aileen Wells Parks. *Thomas Mac-*

Donagh; The Man, The Patriot, The Writer (Athens: University of Georgia Press, 1967), pp. 139-141 [Primary] ; pp. 142-145 [Secondary] .

Willison, I. R., ed. *The New Cambridge Bibliography of English Literature Vol. 4: 1900-1950* (Cambridge: Cambridge University Press, 1972), columns 302-303 [Primary books. Secondary selected] .

McHUGH, Roger (1908-   )

Hogan, Robert. *After the Irish Renaissance; A Critical History of the Irish Drama Since 'The Plough and the Stars'* (Minneapolis: University of Minnesota Press, 1967; London: Macmillan, 1968), p. 266 [Primary books] .

Mac Namara, Brinsley, ed. *Abbey Plays 1899-1948* (Dublin: At the Sign of the Three Candles, [1949]) [Productions at the Abbey Theatre] .

MACKEN, Walter (1915-1967)

Hogan, Robert. *After the Irish Renaissance; A Critical History of the Irish Drama Since 'The Plough and the Stars'* (Minneapolis: University of Minnesota Press, 1967; London: Macmillan, 1968), pp. 266-267 [Primary books] ; pp. 65-70 [Criticism] .

Mac Namara, Brinsley, ed. *Abbey Plays 1899-1948* (Dublin: At the Sign of the Three Candles, [1949]) [Productions at the Abbey Theatre] .

Sahal, N. *Sixty Years of Realistic Irish Drama (1900-1960)* (Bombay: Macmillan, 1971), pp. 185-190 [Plays and criticism] .

McKENNA, James (1933-   )

Hogan, Robert. "The Modern Drama," *Anglo-Irish Literature: A Review of Research,* ed. Richard J. Finneran (New York: Modern Language Association, 1976), p. 552 [Primary].

MacLIAMMÓIR, Michéal (1899-1978)

Breed, Paul F., and Florence M. Sniderman. *Dramatic Criticism Index; A Bibliography of Commentaries on Playwrights from Ibsen to the Avant-Garde* (Detroit, Michigan: Gale Research Company, 1972), p. 397 [Secondary selected].

Hogan, Robert. *After the Irish Renaissance; A Critical History of the Irish Drama Since 'The Plough and the Stars'* (Minneapolis: University of Minnesota Press, 1967; London: Macmillan, 1968), p. 267 [Primary books].

Mac Namara, Brinsley, ed. *Abbey Plays 1899-1948* (Dublin: At the Sign of the Three Candles, [1949]) [Productions at the Abbey Theatre].

Mellown, Elgin W. *A Descriptive Catalogue of the Bibliographies of 20th Century British Poets, Novelists, and Dramatists* (Troy, New York: Whitston Publishing Company, 1978), p. 228 [Primary and secondary bibliographies].

Willison, I. R., ed. *The New Cambridge Bibliography of English Literature, Vol. 4: 1900-1950* (Cambridge: Cambridge University Press, 1972), columns 964-965 [Primary].

MacMAHON, Bryan (1909-   )

Henderson, Joanne L. "Checklist," *Journal of Irish Literature*, I, No. 2 (May 1972), pp. 112-118 [Primary. Secondary selected] .

Hogan, Robert. *After the Irish Renaissance; A Critical History of the Irish Drama Since 'The Plough and the Stars'* (Minneapolis: University of Minnesota Press, 1967; London: Macmillan, 1968), p. 267 [Primary books] ; pp. 70-74 [Criticism] .

Mellown, Elgin W. *A Descriptive Catalogue of the Bibliographies of 20th Century British Poets, Novelists, and Dramatists* (Troy, New York: Whitston Publishing Company, 1978), p. 228 [Primary and secondary bibliographies] .

MacNAMARA, Brinsley [John Weldon] (1890-1963)

Breed, Paul F., and Florence M. Sniderman. *Dramatic Criticism Index; A Bibliography of Commentaries on Playwrights from Ibsen to the Avant-Garde* (Detroit, Michigan: Gale Research Company, 1972), p. 397 [Secondary selected] .

Hogan, Robert. *After the Irish Renaissance; A Critical History of the Irish Drama Since 'The Plough and the Stars'* (Minneapolis: University of Minnesota Press, 1967; London: Macmillan, 1968), p. 267 [Primary books] ; pp. 32-33 [Criticism] .

McDonnell, Michael. "Brinsley MacNamara: A Checklist," *The Journal of Irish Literature*, IV, No. 2 (May 1975), pp. 79-88 [Primary, including manuscripts] .

Mac Namara, Brinsley, ed. *Abbey Plays 1899-1948* (Dublin: At the Sign of the Three Candles, [1949]) [Productions at the Abbey Theatre].

Nicoll, Allardyce. *English Drama 1900-1930; The Beginnings of the Modern Period* (Cambridge: Cambridge University Press, 1973), p. 807 [First productions].

Willison, I. R., ed. *The New Cambridge Bibliography of English Literature, Vol. 4: 1900-1950* (Cambridge: Cambridge University Press, 1972), column 965 [Primary. Secondary selected].

MacNAMARA, Gerald [Harry Morrow] (1866-1958)

Hogan, Robert. "The Modern Drama," *Anglo-Irish Literature: A Review of Research*, ed. Richard J. Finneran (New York: Modern Language Association, 1976), p. 536 [Primary].

Mac Namara, Brinsley, ed. *Abbey Plays 1899-1948* (Dublin: At the Sign of the Three Candles, [1949]) [Productions at the Abbey Theatre].

MacNEICE, Louis (1907-1963)

Armitage, C. M., and N. Clark. *A Bibliography of the Works of Louis MacNeice,* 2nd ed. (London: Kaye & Ward, 1974).

Breed, Paul F., and Florence M. Sniderman. *Dramatic Criticism Index; A Bibliography of Commentaries on Playwrights from Ibsen to the Avant-Garde* (Detroit, Michigan: Gale Research Company, 1972), p. 398 [Secondary selected].

Coleman, Arthur, and Gary R. Tyler. *Drama Criticism, Vol. I: A Checklist of Interpretation Since 1940 of English and American Plays* (Denver, Colorado: Alan Swallow, 1966), p. 122 [Secondary selected].

Daiches, David. *The Present Age After 1920* (London: The Cresset Press, 1958), pp. 226-227 [Primary books].

Kersnowski, Frank L., C. W. Spinks, and Laird Loomis. *A Bibliography of Modern Irish and Anglo-Irish Literature* (San Antonio, Texas: Trinity University Press, 1976), pp. 73-76 [Primary and secondary books].

Longaker, Mark, and Edwin C. Bolles. *Contemporary English Literature* (New York: Appleton-Century-Crofts, 1953), pp. 289-291 [Primary books. Secondary selected].

McKinnon, William T. "Louis MacNeice: A Bibliography," *Bulletin of Bibliography*, XXVII (1970), pp. 51-52, 48, 79-84 [Primary and secondary selected].

Mellown, Elgin W. *A Descriptive Catalogue of the Bibliographies of 20th Century British Poets, Novelists, and Dramatists* (Troy, New York: Whitston Publishing Company, 1978), pp. 228-229 [Primary and secondary bibliographies].

Samples, Gordon. *The Drama Scholars' Index to Plays and Filmscripts; A Guide to Plays and Filmscripts in Selected Anthologies, Series and Periodicals* (Metuchen, New Jersey: Scarecrow Press, 1974), p. 240 [Primary selected].

Smith, Elton Edward. *Louis MacNeice* (New York: Twayne Publishers, 1970), pp. 215-218 [Primary selected]; pp. 218-224 [Secondary].

Temple, Ruth Z., and Martin Tucker. *Twentieth Century British Literature: A Reference Guide and Bibliography* (New York: Frederick Ungar, 1968), p. 201 [Primary books].

Willison, I. R., ed. *The New Cambridge Bibliography of English Literature, Vol. 4: 1900-1950* (Cambridge: Cambridge University Press, 1972), columns 303-305 [Primary. Secondary selected].

McNULTY, Edward (1865-1943)

Hogan, Robert. "The Modern Drama," *Anglo-Irish Literature: A Review of Research,* ed. Richard J. Finneran (New York: Modern Language Association, 1976), pp. 534-535 [Primary books].

Mac Namara, Brinsley, ed. *Abbey Plays 1899-1948* (Dublin: At the Sign of the Three Candles, [1949]) [Productions at the Abbey Theatre].

MANNING, Mary [Mrs. Mark de Wolfe Howe, Jr.] (?1910-   )

Hogan, Robert. *After the Irish Renaissance; A Critical History of the Irish Drama Since 'The Plough and the Stars'* (Minneapolis: University of Minnesota Press, 1967; London: Macmillan, 1968), p. 267 [Primary books]; pp. 119-122 [Criticism].

MARTYN, Edward (1859-1923)

Adelman, Irving, and Rita Dworkin. *Modern Drama; A Checklist of Critical Literature on 20th Century Plays* (Metuchen, New Jersey: Scarecrow Press, 1967), pp. 192-193 [Secondary selected].

Breed, Paul F., and Florence M. Sniderman. *Dramatic Criticism Index; A Bibliography of Commentaries on Play-*

wrights from Ibsen to the Avant-Garde (Detroit, Michigan: Gale Research Company, 1972), pp. 410-412 [Secondary selected].

Coleman, Arthur, and Gary R. Tyler. *Drama Criticism. Vol. I: A Checklist of Interpretation Since 1940 of English and American Plays* (Denver, Colorado: Alan Swallow, 1966), p. 135 [Secondary selected].

Courtney, Sister Marie-Thérèse. *Edward Martyn and the Irish Theatre* (New York: Vantage Press, 1956), pp. 172-188 [Primary and secondary].

Hogan, Robert. "The Modern Drama," *Anglo-Irish Literature: A Review of Research,* ed. Richard J. Finneran (New York: Modern Language Association, 1976), p. 535 [Primary books. Secondary selected].

Kersnowski, Frank L., C. W. Spinks, and Laird Loomis. *A Bibliography of Modern Irish and Anglo-Irish Literature* (San Antonio, Texas: Trinity University Press, 1976), pp. 80-81 [Primary and secondary books].

Lauterbach, Edward S., and W. Eugene Davis. *The Transitional Age: British Literature 1880-1920* (Troy, New York: Whitston Publishing Company, 1973), p. 218 [Primary books. Secondary selected].

Mac Namara, Brinsley, ed. *Abbey Plays 1899-1948* (Dublin: At the Sign of the Three Candles, [1949]) [Productions at the Abbey Theatre].

Mellown, Elgin W. *A Descriptive Catalogue of the Bibliographies of 20th Century British Poets, Novelists and Dramatists* (Troy, New York: Whitston Publishing Company, 1978), pp. 234-235 [Primary and secondary bibliographies].

Nicoll, Allardyce. *English Drama 1900-1930; The Beginnings of the Modern Period* (Cambridge: Cambridge University Press, 1973), p. 819 [First productions].

Watson, George, ed. *The New Cambridge Bibliography of*

English Literature, Vol. 3: 1800-1900 (Cambridge: Cambridge University Press, 1969), column 1939 [Primary books. Secondary selected] .

MAYNE, Rutherford [Samuel J. Waddell] (1878-   ?)

Breed, Paul F., and Florence M. Sniderman. *Dramatic Criticism Index; A Bibliography of Commentaries on Playwrights from Ibsen to the Avant-Garde* (Detroit, Michigan: Gale Research Company, 1972), p. 419 [Secondary selected] .

Hogan, Robert. "The Modern Drama," *Anglo-Irish Literature: A Review of Research,* ed. Richard J. Finneran (New York: Modern Language Association, 1976), p. 540 [Primary. Secondary selected] .

Kersnowski, Frank L., C. W. Spinks, and Laird Loomis. *A Bibliography of Modern Irish and Anglo-Irish Literature* (San Antonio, Texas: Trinity University Press, 1976), pp. 81-82 [Primary books] .

Mac Namara, Brinsley, ed. *Abbey Plays 1899-1948* (Dublin: At the Sign of the Three Candles, [1949]) [Productions at the Abbey Theatre] .

Mellown, Elgin W. *A Descriptive Catalogue of the Bibliographies of 20th Century British Poets, Novelists, and Dramatists* (Troy, New York: Whitston Publishing Company, 1978), p. 239 [Primary and secondary bibliographies] .

Nicoll, Allardyce. *English Drama 1900-1930; The Beginnings of the Modern Period* (Cambridge: Cambridge University Press, 1973), p. 827 [First productions] .

Watson, George, ed. *The New Cambridge Bibliography of English Literature, Vol. 3: 1800-1900* (Cambridge: Cambridge University Press, 1969), column 1941 [Primary books. Secondary selected] .

MELDON, Maurice (1928-1958)

Hogan, Robert. *After the Irish Renaissance; A Critical History of the Irish Drama Since 'The Plough and the Stars'* (Minneapolis: University of Minnesota Press, 1967; London: Macmillan, 1968), p. 268 [Primary books] ; pp. 226-229 [Criticism] .

MILLIGAN, Alice (1866-1953)

Hogan, Robert. "The Modern Drama," *Anglo-Irish Literature: A Review of Research,* ed. Richard J. Finneran (New York: Modern Language Association, 1976), p. 536 [Primary. Secondary selected] .

Mac Namara, Brinsley, ed. *Abbey Plays 1899-1948* (Dublin: At the Sign of the Three Candles, [1949]) [Productions at the Abbey Theatre] .

Nicoll, Allardyce. *English Drama 1900-1930; The Beginnings of the Modern Period* (Cambridge: Cambridge University Press, 1973), p. 835 [First productions] .

Robinson, Lennox. *Ireland's Abbey Theatre; A History 1899-1951* (London: Sidgwick & Jackson, 1951), pp. 13, 15 [Primary and criticism] .

MOLLOY, Michael J. (1917-   )

Breed, Paul F., and Florence M. Sniderman. *Dramatic Criticism Index; A Bibliography of Commentaries on Playwrights from Ibsen to the Avant-Garde* (Detroit, Michigan: Gale Research Company, 1972), p. 440 [Secondary selected].

Hogan, Robert. *After the Irish Renaissance; A Critical History of the Irish Drama Since 'The Plough and the Stars'* (Minneapolis: University of Minnesota Press, 1967; London: Macmillan, 1968), p. 268 [Primary]; pp. 86-89 [Criticism].

Mac Namara, Brinsley, ed. *Abbey Plays 1899-1948* (Dublin: at the Sign of the Three Candles, [1949]) [Productions at the Abbey Theatre].

Sahal, N. *Sixty Years of Realistic Irish Drama (1900-1960)* (Bombay: Macmillan, 1971), pp. 176-185 [Plays and criticism].

MOORE, George (1852-1933)

Batho, Edith, and Bonamy Dobrée. *The Victorians and After 1830-1914.* Introductions to English Literature IV, ed. Bonamy Dobrée (London: The Cresset Press, 1938), pp. 316-317 [Primary books].

Breed, Paul F., and Florence M. Sniderman. *Dramatic Criticism Index; A Bibliography of Commentaries on Playwrights from Ibsen to the Avant-Garde* (Detroit, Michigan: Gale Research Company, 1972), pp. 447-448 [Secondary selected].

Coleman, Arthur, and Gary R. Tyler. *Drama Criticism, Vol. I: A Checklist of Interpretation Since 1940 of English and American Plays* (Denver, Colorado: Alan Swallow, 1966), p. 152 [Secondary selected].

Collet, George Paul. *Moore et la France* (Geneva: Droz; Paris: Minard, 1957) [Lists uncollected articles and prefaces].

Cutler, Bradley D., and Villa Stiles. *Modern British Authors: Their First Editions* (Greenberg: G. Allen, 1930; Folcroft, Pennsylvania: Folcroft Press, 1969), pp. 118-121 [Primary].

Danielson, Henry. "Moore: A Bibliography 1878-1921," in John Freeman, *A Portrait of Moore in a Study of His Work* (London: Werner Laurie, 1922) [Primary].

Gerber, Helmut E. "George Moore: An Annotated Bibliography of Writings about Him," *English Fiction in Transition,* II, No. 2 (1959), pp. 1-91. Supplemented in subsequent issues of *English Fiction* [later *English Literature*] in *Transition* [Secondary].

—. "George Moore," *Anglo-Irish Literature: A Review of Research,* ed. Richard J. Finneran (New York: Modern Language Association, 1976), pp. 138-166 [Secondary annotated].

Gilcher, Edwin. *A Bibliography of George Moore* (De Kalb, Illinois: Northern Illinois University Press, 1970) [Primary annotated].

—. *Books and Other Printed Items by George Moore in the Library of Edwin Gilcher* (Cherry Plain: Privately printed, 1974).

Kersnowski, Frank L., C. W. Spinks, and Laird Loomis. *A Bibliography of Modern Irish and Anglo-Irish Literature* (San Antonio, Texas: Trinity University Press, 1976), p. 85 [Bibliographies].

Lauterbach, Edward S., and W. Eugene Davis. *The Transitional Age: British Literature 1800-1920* (Troy, New York: Whitston Publishing Company, 1973), pp. 225-228 [Primary books. Secondary selected].

Longaker, Mark, and Edwin C. Bolles. *Contemporary English*

Literature (New York: Appleton-Century-Crofts 1953), pp. 203-207 [Primary books. Secondary selected].

Mac Namara, Brinsley, ed. *Abbey Plays 1899-1948* (Dublin: At the Sign of the Three Candles, [1949]) [Productions at the Abbey Theatre].

Mellown, Elgin W. *A Descriptive Catalogue of the Bibliographies of 20th Century British Poets, Novelsits, and Dramatists* (Troy, New York: Whitston Publishing Company, 1978), pp. 248-249 [Primary and secondary bibliographies].

Millett, Fred B. *Contemporary British Literature; A Critical Survey and 232 Author Bibliographies* (New York: Harcourt, Brace, 1935), pp. 371-374 [Primary books. Secondary selected].

Nicoll, Allardyce. *English Drama 1900-1930; The Beginnings of the Modern Period* (Cambridge: Cambridge University Press, 1973), p. 842 [First productions].

Noël, Jean C. *George Moore; L'homme et l'oeuvre (1852-1933)* (Paris: Marcel Didier, 1966), pp. 555-603 [Primary]; pp. 604-647 [Secondary selected].

Temple, Ruth Z., and Martin Tucker. *Twentieth Century British Literature: A Reference Guide and Bibliography* (New York: Frederick Ungar, 1968), pp. 207-208 [Primary books. Secondary selected].

Watson, George, ed. *The New Cambridge Bibliography of English Literature, Vol. 3: 1800-1900* (Cambridge: Cambridge University Press, 1969), columns 1014-1019 [Primary books. Secondary selected].

Williams, I. A. *Bibliographies of Modern Authors. No. 3: George Moore* (London: Chaundy, 1921) [Pamphet].

MURPHY, John (-   )

Hogan, Robert. *After the Irish Renaissance; A Critical History of the Irish Drama Since 'The Plough and the Stars'* (Minneapolis: University of Minnesota Press, 1967; London: Macmillan, 1968), p. 268 [Primary books] ; pp. 81-82 [Criticism] .

MURPHY, Thomas (1935-   )

Armstrong, William A. *Experimental Drama* (London: G. Bell, 1963), pp. 99-101 [Primary works. Criticism] .

Elsom, John. "Thomas Murphy," *Contemporary Dramatists,* ed. James Vinson (London: St. James Press; New York: St. Martin's Press, 1973), pp. 566-567 [Primary] ; pp. 567-569 [Criticism] .

Hogan, Robert. "The Modern Drama," *Anglo-Irish Literature: A Review of Research,* ed. Richard J. Finneran (New York: Modern Language Association, 1976), p. 552 [Primary. Secondary selected] .

MURRAY, T[homas] C[ornelius] (1873-1959)

Adelman, Irving, and Rita Dworkin. *Modern Drama; A Checklist of Critical Literature on 20th Century Plays* (Metuchen, New Jersey: Scarecrow Press, 1967), p. 205 [Secondary selected] .

Breed, Paul F., and Florence M. Sniderman. *Dramatic Criticism Index; A Bibliography of Commentaries on Playwrights from Ibsen to the Avant-Garde* (Detroit, Michigan: Gale Research Company, 1972), pp. 451-452 [Secondary selected] .

Coleman, Arthur, and Gary R. Tyler. *Drama Criticism, Vol. I: A Checklist of Interpretation Since 1940 of English and American Plays* (Denver, Colorado: Alan Swallow, 1966), p. 153 [Secondary selected].

Hogan, Robert. "The Modern Drama," *Anglo-Irish Literature: A Review of Research,* ed. Richard J. Finneran (New York: Modern Language Association, 1976), p. 537 [Primary. Secondary selected].

Kersnowski, Frank L., C. W. Spinks, and Laird Loomis. *A Bibliography of Modern Irish and Anglo-Irish Literature* (San Antonio, Texas: Trinity University Press, 1976), pp. 86-87 [Primary books].

Lauterbach, Edward S., and W. Eugene Davis. *The Transitional Age: British Literature 1880-1920* (Troy, New York: Whitston Publishing Company, 1973), pp. 232-233 [Primary books. Secondary selected].

Mac Namara, Brinsley, ed. *Abbey Plays 1899-1948* (Dublin: At the Sign of the Three Candles, [1949]) [Productions at the Abbey Theatre].

Mellown, Elgin W. *A Descriptive Catalogue of the Bibliographies of 20th Century British Poets, Novelists, and Dramatists* (Troy, New York: Whitston Publishing Company, 1978), p. 258 [Primary and secondary bibliographies].

Millett, Fred B. *Contemporary British Literature: A Critical Survey and 232 Author Bibliographies* (New York: Harcourt, Brace, 1935), p. 385 [Primary books. Secondary selected].

Nicoll, Allardyce. *English Drama 1900-1930; The Beginnings of the Modern Period* (Cambridge: Cambridge University Press, 1973), pp. 851-852 [First productions].

Salem, James M. *A Guide to Critical Reviews. Part III: British and Continental Drama from Ibsen to Pinter* (Metuchen, New Jersey: Scarecrow Press, 1968), pp. 173-174 [Secondary selected].

Watson, George, ed. *The New Cambridge Bibliography of English Literature, Vol. 3: 1800-1900* (Cambridge: Cambridge University Press, 1969), columns 1944-1945 [Primary books. Secondary selected].

O'BRIEN, Conor Cruise [Donat O'Donnell] (1917-   )

Henderson, Joanne L. "A Conor Cruise O'Brien Checklist," in Elisabeth Young-Bruehl and Robert Hogan. *Conor Cruise O'Brien: An Appraisal* (Newark, Delaware: Prescenium Press, 1974), pp. 49-64 [Primary. Secondary selected].

O'BRIEN, Flann. See O'NOLAN, Brian

O'BRIEN, Kate (1897-1974)

Hogan, Robert. "The Modern Drama," *Anglo-Irish Literature: A Review of Research*, ed. Richard J. Finneran (New York: Modern Language Association, 1976), p. 544 [Primary books].

Mellown, Elgin W. *A Descriptive Catalogue of the Bibliographies of 20th Century British Poets, Novelists, and Dramatists* (Troy, New York: Whitston Publishing Company, 1978), p. 266 [Primary and secondary bibliographies].

Willison, I. R., ed. *The New Cambridge Bibliography of English Literature, Vol. 4: 1900-1950* (Cambridge: Cambridge University Press, 1972), columns 683-684 [Primary books. Secondary selected] .

O'CASEY, Sean (1880-1964)

Adelman, Irving, and Rita Dworkin. *Modern Drama; A Checklist of Critical Literature on 20th Century Plays* (Metuchen, New Jersey: Scarecrow Press, 1967), pp. 206-210 [Secondary selected] .

Armstrong, William A. *Sean O'Casey.* Writers and Their Works, 198. Second Edition (London: Longmans, Green, 1971), pp. 33-38 [Primary. Secondary selected] .

Ayling, Ronald, ed. *Sean O'Casey.* Modern Judgements Series (London: Macmillan, 1969), pp. 261-269 [Primary books. Secondary selected] .

—. "A Note on Sean O'Casey's Manuscripts and His Working Methods," *Bulletin of the New York Public Library,* (June 1969), pp. 359-367 [A bibliographical article introducing the O'Casey manuscripts acquired by the Berg Collection in the New York Public Library] .

—. "Sean O'Casey," *The New Cambridge Bibliography of English Literature,* Volume 4: 1900-1950, ed. I. R. Willison (Cambridge: Cambridge University Press, 1972), columns 879-885 [Primary. Secondary selected] .

—. "Detailed Catalogue of Sean O'Casey's Papers at the Time of His Death," *The Sean O'Casey Review,* I, No. 2 (Spring 1975), pp. 48-65; II, No. 1 (Fall 1975), pp. 64-77; III, No. 1 (Fall 1976), pp. 58-70.

—, and Michael J. Durkan. "Work by Sean O'Casey in Translation," *The Sean O'Casey Review,* I, No. 2 (Spring 1975), pp. 4-18; II, No. 1 (Fall 1975), pp. 5-11 [Translations in 25 languages] .

—, and Michael J. Durkan. *Sean O'Casey: A Bibliography*

(London: Macmillan, 1978) [Primary].

Brandstädter, Otto. "Ein O'Casey-Bibliographie," *Zeitschrift fur Anglistik und Amerikanistik* (Berlin), II (1954), pp. 240-254 [Secondary].

Breed, Paul F., and Florence M. Sniderman. *Dramatic Criticism Index; A Bibliography of Commentaries on Playwrights from Ibsen to the Avant-Garde* (Detroit, Michigan: Gale Research Company, 1972), pp. 459-470 [Secondary selected].

Carpenter, Charles A. "Sean O'Casey Studies Through 1964," *Modern Drama*, X, No. 1 (May 1967), pp. 17-23 [Secondary].

Coleman, Arthur, and Gary R. Tyler. *Drama Criticism, Vol. I: A Checklist of Interpretation Since 1940 of English and American Plays* (Denver, Colorado: Alan Swallow, 1966), pp. 154-156 [Secondary selected].

Cowasjee, Saros. *Sean O'Casey: The Man Behind the Plays* (Edinburgh and London: Oliver & Boyd, 1963; New York: St. Martin's Press, 1964; revised ed. 1965), pp. 256-261 [Secondary selected].

—. *O'Casey* (Edinburgh and London: Oliver & Boyd, 1966; New York: Barnes & Noble, 1967), pp. 116-120 [Secondary selected].

Dumay, E. J. "A Comprehensive List of O'Casey Productions in France (1947-1975)," *The Sean O'Casey Review*, III, No. 1 (Fall 1976), pp. 37-38 [Includes name of play, theatre, director, and year].

Kersnowski, Frank L., C. W. Spinks, and Laird Loomis. *A Bibliography of Modern Irish and Anglo-Irish Literature* (San Antonio, Texas: Trinity University Press, 1976), pp. 87-91 [Primary and secondary books].

Kosok, Heinz. *Sean O'Casey; Das Dramatische Werk* (Berlin: Erich Schmidt, 1972), pp. 397-413 [Secondary selected].

Krause, David. "Sean O'Casey," *Anglo-Irish Literature, A Review of Research,* ed. Richard J. Finneran (New Yrok: Modern Language Association, 1976), pp. 470-517 [Secondary annotated] .

Levidova, I. M., and V. M. Parchevskaia. *Sean O'Casey Bibliographic Guide.* Writers of Foreign Countries Series (Moscow: Knigna Publishing House, 1964) [Primary and secondary. In Russian] .

Longaker, Mark, and Edwin C. Bolles. *Contemporary English Literature* (New York: Appleton-Century-Crofts, 1953), p. 64 [Primary books] .

Lowery, Robert G. "Premieres and Casts of Sean O'Casey's Plays," *The Sean O'Casey Review,* II, No. 1 (Fall 1975), pp. 23-37 [Includes name of play, theatre, director, and date] .

Mac Namara, Brinsley, ed. *Abbey Plays 1899-1948* (Dublin: At the Sign of the Three Candles, [1949]) [Productions at the Abbey Theatre] .

Mellown, Elgin W. *A Descriptive Catalogue of the Bibliographies of 20th Century British Poets, Novelists, and Dramatists* (Troy, New York: Whitston Publishing Company, 1978), pp. 266-268 [Primary and secondary bibliographies] .

Metscher, Thomas. *Sean O'Caseys Dramatischer Stil* (Braunschweig: Georg Westermann, 1968), pp. 11-18 [Secondary selected] .

Mikhail, E. H. *Sean O'Casey: A Bibliography of Criticism* (London: Macmillan, 1972) [Primary books. Secondary] .

—. "Sean O'Casey Studies: An Annual Bibliography," *The Sean O'Casey Review,* III, No. 1 (Fall 1976) to the present [Supplements the author's *Sean O'Casey: A Bibliography of Criticism*] .

Nicoll, Allardyce. *English Drama 1900-1930; The Beginnings of the Modern Period* (Cambridge: Cambridge University Press, 1973), pp. 860-861 [First productions].

Palmer, Helen H., and Anne Jane Dyson. *European Drama Criticism* (Hamden, Connecticut: Shoe String Press, 1968), pp. 300-305; *Supplement* I (1970), pp. 130-132; *Supplement* II (1974), pp. 116-117 [Secondary selected].

Salem, James M. *A Guide To Critical Reviews. Part III: British and Continental Drama from Ibsen to Pinter* (Metuchen, New Jersey: Scarecrow Press, 1968), pp. 174-178 [Secondary selected].

Samples, Gordon. *The Drama Scholars' Index to Plays and Filmscripts; A Guide to Plays and Filmscripts in Selected Anthologies, Series and Periodicals* (Metuchen, New Jersey: Scarecrow Press, 1974), p. 282 [Primary selected].

Temple, Ruth Z., and Martin Tucker. *Twentieth Century British Literature: A Reference Guide and Bibliography* (New York: Frederick Ungar, 1968), p. 213 [Primary books].

O'CONNOR, Frank [Michael O'Donovan] (1903-1966)

Breed, Paul F., and Florence M. Sniderman. *Dramatic Criticism Index; A Bibliography of Commentaries on Playwrights from Ibsen to the Avant-Garde* (Detroit, Michigan: Gale Research Company, 1972), p. 470 [Secondary selected].

Brenner, Gerry. "Frank O'Connor, 1903-1966: A Bibliography," *West Coast Review,* II, No. 2 (1967), pp. 55-64 [Primary and secondary].

Kersnowski, Frank L., C. W. Spinks, and Laird Loomis. *A Bibliography of Modern Irish and Anglo-Irish Literature* (San Antonio, Texas: Trinity University Press, 1976), pp. 91-94 [Primary and secondary books] .

Mac Namara, Brinsley, ed. *Abbey Plays 1899-1948* (Dublin: At the Sign of the Three Candles, [1949]) [Productions at the Abbey Theatre] .

Matthews, James H. "Selected Bibliography," *Frank O'Connor* (Lewisburg, Pennsylvania: Bucknell University Press, 1976), pp. 91-94 [Primary and secondary] .

Mellown, Elgin W. *A Descriptive Catalogue of the Bibliographies of 20th Century British Poets, Novelists, and Dramatists* (Troy, New York: Whitston Publishing Company, 1978), pp. 268-269 [Primary and secondary bibliographies] .

Samples, Gordon. *The Drama Scholars' Index to Plays and Filmscripts; A Guide to Plays and Filmscripts in Selected Anthologies, Series and Periodicals* (Metuchen, New Jersey: Scarecrow Press, 1974), p. 283 [Primary selected] .

Temple, Ruth Z., and Martin Tucker. *Twentieth Century British Literature: A Reference Guide and Bibliography* (New York: Frederick Ungar, 1968), pp. 213-214 [Primary books] .

Willison, I. R., ed. *The New Cambridge Bibliography of English Literature, Vol 4: 1900-1950* (Cambridge: Cambridge University Press, 1972), columns 684-685 [Primary books. Secondary selected] .

O'CONNOR, Joseph (1916-   )

Hogan, Robert. *After the Irish Renaissance; A Critical History of the Irish Drama Since 'The Plough and the Stars'* (Minneapolis: University of Minnesota Press, 1967; London: Macmillan, 1968), p. 269 [Primary books] .

Samples, Gordon. *The Drama Scholars' Index to Plays and*

Filmscripts; A Guide to Plays and Filmscripts in Selected Anthologies, Series and Periodicals (Metuchen, New Jersey: Scarecrow Press, 1974), p. 282 [Primary selected].

O'DONNELL, Frank J. Hugh (-   )

Breed, Paul F., and Florence M. Sniderman. *Dramatic Criticism Index; A Bibliography of Commentaries on Playwrights from Ibsen to the Avant-Garde* (Detroit, Michigan: Gale Research Company, 1972), p. 476 [Secondary selected].

Mac Namara, Brinsley, ed. *Abbey Plays 1899-1948* (Dublin: At the Sign of the Three Candles, [1949]) [Productions at the Abbey Theatre].

Nicoll, Allardyce. *English Drama 1900-1930; The Beginnings of the Modern Period* (Cambridge: Cambridge University Press, 1973), p. 861 [First productions].

O'DONNELL, Peadar (1893-   )

Freyer, Grattan. "Bibliography," *Peadar O'Donnell.* Irish Writers Series (Lewisburg, Pennsylvania: Bucknell University Press, 1973), pp. 125-128 [Primary. Secondary selected].

Mac Namara, Brinsley, ed. *Abbey Plays 1899-1948* (Dublin: At the Sign of the Three Candles, [1949]) [Productions at the Abbey Theatre].

Mellown, Elgin W. *A Descriptive Catalogue of the Bibliographies of 20th Century British Poets, Novelists, and Dramatists* (Troy, New York: Whitston Publishing Company, 1978), p. 269 [Primary and secondary bibliogra-

phies] .

O'DONOVAN, Harry (　　-　　)

Hogan, Robert. *After the Irish Renaissance; A Critical History of the Irish Drama Since 'The Plough and the Stars'* (Minneapolis: University of Minnesota Press, 1967; London: Macmillan, 1968), p. 269 [Primary books] .

O'DONOVAN, John (1921-　　)

Hogan, Robert. *After the Irish Renaissance; A Critical History of the Irish Drama Since 'The Plough and the Stars'* (Minneapolis: University of Minnesota Press, 1967; London: Macmillan, 1968), p. 269 [Primary books] ; pp. 77-81 [Criticism] .

O'DUFFY, Eimar (1893-1935)

Hogan, Robert. "Bibliography," *Eimar O'Duffy.* Irish Writers Series (Lewisburg, Pennsylvania: Bucknell University Press, 1972), pp. 82-84 [Primary books. Secondary selected] .

Kersnowski, Frank L., C. W. Spinks, and Laird Loomis. *A Bibliography of Modern Irish and Anglo-Irish Literature* (San Antonio, Texas: Trinity University Press, 1976), pp. 94-96 [Primary and secondary books] .

MacLochlainn, Alf. "Eimar O'Duffy: A Bibliographical Biography," *Irish Book,* I (Winter 1959-1960), pp. 37-46

[Primary] .

Mellown, Elgin W. *A Descriptive Catalogue of the Bibliographies of 20th Century British Poets, Novelists, and Dramatists* (Troy, New York: Whitston Publishing Company, 1978), pp. 269-270 [Primary and secondary bibliographies] .

Nicoll, Allardyce. *English Drama 1900-1930; The Beginnings of the Modern Period* (Cambridge: Cambridge University Press, 1973), p. 861 [First productions] .

O'FAOLÁIN, Seán (1900-   )

Daiches, David. *The Present Age After 1920* (London: The Cresset Press, 1958), p. 306 [Primary books] .

Doyle, Paul A. *Sean O'Faolain* (New York: Twayne Publishers, 1968), pp. 143-147 [Primary] ; pp. 148-152 [Secondart selected] .

Harmon, Maurice. *Sean O'Faolain; A Critical Introduction* (Notre Dame and London: University of Notre Dame Press, 1967), pp. 203-213 [Primary] ; pp. 216-217 [Secondary] .

Kersnowski, Frank L., C. W. Spinks, and Laird Loomis. *A Bibliography of Modern Irish and Anglo-Irish Literature* (San Antonio, Texas: Trinity University Press, 1976), pp. 96-98 [Primary and secondary books] .

Mac Namara, Brinsley, ed. *Abbey Plays 1899-1948* (Dublin: At the Sign of the Three Candles, [1949]) [Productions at the Abbey Theatre] .

Mellown, Elgin W. *A Descriptive Catalogue of the Bibliographies of 20th Century British Poets, Novelists, and Dramatists* (Troy, New York: Whitston Publishing Company, 1978), p. 270 [Primary and secondary bibliogra-

phies] .

Millett, Fred B. *Contemporary British Literature; A Critical Survey and 232 Author Bibliographies* (New York: Harcourt, Brance, 1935), p. 400 [Primary books. Secondary selected] .

Temple, Ruth Z., and Martin Tucker. *Twentieth Century British Literature: A Reference Guide and Bibliography* (New York: Frederick Ungar, 1968), p. 214 [Primary books] .

Willison, I. R., ed. *The New Cambridge Bibliography of English Literature, Vol. 4: 1900-1950* (Cambridge: Cambridge University Press, 1972), columns 685-686 [Primary books. Secondary selected] .

O'FARACHÁIN, Roibeárd (1909-   )

Hogan, Robert. "The Modern Drama," *Anglo-Irish Literature: A Review of Research,* ed. Richard J. Finneran (New York: Modern Language Association, 1976), p. 548 [Primary] .

Mac Namara, Brinsley, ed. *Abbey Plays 1899-1948* (Dublin: At the Sign of the Three Candles, [1949]) [Productions at the Abbey Theatre] .

O'FLAHERTY, Liam (1897-   )

Doyle, Paul. "Liam O'Flaherty Checklist," *Twentieth Century Literature,* XIII (1967), pp. 49-51 [Primary. Secondary selected] .

—. *Liam O'Flaherty; An Annotated Bibliography* (Troy,

New York: Whitston Publishing Company, 1972) [Primary and secondary].

Gawsworth, John. *Ten Contemporaries; Notes Toward Their Definitive Bibliography.* Second Series (London: Joiner and Steele, 1933), pp. 144-160 [Primary books 1923-1932, with bibliographical notes].

Mellown, Elgin W. *A Descriptive Catalogue of the Bibliographies of 20th Century British Poets, Novelists, and Dramatists* (Troy, New York: Whitston Publishing Company, 1978), p. 271 [Primary and secondary bibliographies].

Willison, I. R., ed. *The New Cambridge Bibliography of English Literature, Vol. 4: 1900-1950* (Cambridge: Cambridge University Press, 1972), columns 686-687 [Primary books. Secondary selected].

O'KELLY, Seumas (1881-1918)

Breed, Paul F., and Florence M. Sniderman. *Dramatic Criticism Index; A Bibliography of Commentaries on Playwrights from Ibsen to the Avant-Garde* (Detroit, Michigan: Gale Research Company, 1972), pp. 476-477 [Secondary selected].

Hogan, Robert. "The Modern Drama," *Anglo-Irish Literature: A Review of Research,* ed. Richard J. Finneran (New York: Modern Language Association, 1976), pp. 538-539 [Primary. Secondary selected].

Kersnowski, Frank L., C. W. Spinks, and Laird Loomis. *A Bibliography of Modern Irish and Anglo-Irish Literature* (San Antonio, Texas: Trinity University Press, 1976), pp. 105-107 [Primary and secondary books].

Mac Namara, Brinsley, ed. *Abbey Plays 1899-1948* (Dublin: At the Sign of the Three Candles, [1949]) [Productions at the Abbey Theatre] .

Mellown, Elgin W. *A Descriptive Catalogue of the Bibliographies of 20th Century British Poets, Novelists, and Dramatists* (Troy, New York: Whitston Publishing Company, 1978), p. 273 [Primary bibliographies] .

Nicoll, Allardyce. *English Drama 1900-1930; The Beginnings of the Modern Period* (Cambridge: Cambridge University Press, 1973), p. 862 [First productions] .

O'Hegarty, Patrick Sarsfield. "Bibliographies of 1916 and the Irish Revolution, IV. Seamus O'Kelly," *Dublin Magazine*, IX (October-December 1934), pp. 47-51 [Primary books, with bibliographical notes] .

Saul, G. B. "Bibliographies," *Seumas O'Kelly*. Irish Writers Series (Lewisburg, Pennsylvania: Bucknell University Press, 1971), pp. 81-101 [Primary annotated. Secondary selected] .

Willison, I. R. ed. *The New Cambridge Bibliography of English Literature, Vol. 4: 1900-1950* (Cambridge: Cambridge University Press, 1972), columns 687-688 [Primary] .

O'NEILL, Seamus (-   )

Hogan, Robert. *After the Irish Renaissance; A Critical History of the Irish Drama Since 'The Plough and the Stars'* (Minneapolis: University of Minnesota Press, 1967; London: Macmillan, 1968), p. 269 [Primary books] .

O'NOLAN, Brian [Wrote under pseudonyms Flann O'Brien and Myles Na Gopaleen] (1912-1965)

Clissmann, Anne. *Flann O'Brien; A Critical Introduction to His Writings* (Dublin: Gill & Macmillan; New York: Barnes & Noble, 1975), pp. 359-365 [Secondary selected] .

Hogan, Robert. "The Modern Drama," *Anglo-Irish Literature: A Review of Research,* ed. Richard J. Finneran (New York: Modern Language Association, 1976), p. 549 [Primary. Secondary selected] .

Kersnowski, Frank L., C. W. Spinks, and Laird Loomis. *A Bibliography of Modern Irish and Anglo-Irish Literature* (San Antonio, Texas: Trinity University Press, 1976), pp. 107-108 [Primary and secondary books] .

Mellown, Elgin W. *A Descriptive Catalogue of the Bibliographies of 20th Century British Poets, Novelists, and Dramatists* (Troy, New York: Whitston Publishing Company, 1978), pp. 274-275 [Primary and secondary bibliographies] .

O'Keefe, Timothy, ed.   "Bibliographical Notes," *Myles: Portraits of Brian O'Nolan* (London: Martin Brian & O'Keefe, 1973), pp. 122-134 [Primary and secondary selected] .

Powell, David. "A Checklist of Brian O'Nolan," *The Journal of Irish Literature,* III, No. 1 (January 1974), pp. 104-112 [Primary. Secondary selected] .

Willison, I. R., ed. *The New Cambridge Bibliography of English Literature, Vol. 4: 1900-1950* (Cambridge: Cambridge University Press, 1972), column 683 [Primary] .

O'RIORDAN, Conal Holmes O'Connell [Norreys Connell] (1874-1948)

Bateson, F. W., ed. *The Cambridge Bibliography of English Literature, Vol. III: 1800-1900* (Cambridge: Cambridge University Press, 1940), column 1965 [Primary books].

Breed, Paul F., and Florence M. Sniderman. *Dramatic Criticism Index; A Bibliography of Commentaries on Playwrights from Ibsen to the Avent-Garde* (Detroit, Michigan: Gale Reserach Company, 1972), p. 523 [Secondary selected].

Hogan, Robert. "The Modern Drama," *Anglo-Irish Literature: A Review of Research,* ed. Richard J. Finneran (New York: Modern Language Association, 1976), pp. 535-536 [Primary].

Kersnowski, Frank L., C. W. Spinks, and Laird Loomis. *A Bibliography of Modern Irish and Anglo-Irish Literature* (San Antonio, Texas: Trinity University Press, 1976), pp. 108-109 [Primary books].

Longaker, Mark, and Edwin C. Bolles. *Contemporary English Literature* (New York: Appleton-Century-Crofts, 1953), pp. 62-63 [Primary books].

Mac Namara, Brinsley, ed. *Abbey Plays 1899-1948* (Dublin: At the Sign of the Three Candles, [1949]) [Productions at the Abbey Theatre].

Mellown, Elgin, W. *A Descriptive Catalogue of the Bibliographies of 20th Century British Poets, Novelists, and Dramatists* (Troy, New York: Whitston Publishing Company, 1978), p. 276 [Secondary bibliographies].

Millett, Fred B. *Contemporary British Literature; A Critical Survey and 232 Author Bibliographies* (New York: Harcourt, Brace, 1935), pp. 406-407 [Primary books. Secondary selected].

Nicoll, Allardyce. *English Drama 1900-1930; The Beginnings of the Modern Period* (Cambridge: Cambridge University

Press, 1973), p. 866 [First productions].

PEARSE, Pádraic (1879-1916)

Hogan, Robert. "The Modern Drama," *Anglo-Irish Literature: A Review of Research*, ed. Richard J. Finneran (New York: Modern Language Association, 1976), p. 540 [Primary. Secondary selected].

Mac Namara, Brinsley, ed. *Abbey Plays 1899-1948* (Dublin: At the Sign of the Three Candles, [1949]) [Productions at the Abbey Theatre].

Mellown, Elgin W. *A Descriptive Catalogue of the Bibliographies of 20th Century British Poets, Novelists, and Dramatists* (Troy, New York: Whitston Publishing Company, 1978), p. 282 [Primary and secondary bibliographies].

O'Hegarty, P. S. "Bibliographies of 1916 and the Irish Revolution, 1. Padraic Henry Pearse," *The Dublin Magazine*, VI (July-September 1931), pp. 44-49 [Primary books, with bibliographical notes].

PLUNKETT [Kelly], James (1920-   )

Hogan, Robert. "The Modern Drama," *Anglo-Irish Literature: A Review of Research*, ed. Richard J. Finneran (New York: Modern Language Association, 1976), p. 550 [Primary].

RAY, R. J. [R. J. Brophy] (c. 1865-   )

Mac Namara, Brinsley, ed. *Abbey Plays 1899-1948* (Dublin: At the Sign of the Three Candles, [1949]) [Productions at the Abbey Theatre].

Malone, Andrew E. *The Irish Drama* (London: Constable; New York: Scribner's, 1929), pp. 104, 273 [Plays and criticism].

Nicoll, Allardyce. *English Drama 1900-1930; The Beginnings of the Modern Period* (Cambridge: Cambridge University Press, 1973), p. 904 [First productions].

Robinson, Lennox. *Ireland's Abbey Theatre; A History 1899-1951* (London: Sidgwick & Jackson, 1951), pp. 81, 90 [Plays and criticism].

Sahal, N. *Sixty Years of Realistic Irish Drama (1900-1960)* (Bombay: Macmillan, 1971), pp. 46-48 [Plays and criticism].

ROBINSON, [Esmé Stuart] Lennox (1886-1958)

Breed, Paul F., and Florence M. Sniderman. *Dramatic Criticism Index; A Bibliography of Commentaries on Playwrights from Ibsen to the Avant-Garde* (Detroit, Michigan: Gale Research Company, 1972), pp. 565-566 [Secondary selected].

Kersnowski, Frank L., C. W. Spinks, and Laird Loomis. *A Bibliography of Modern Irish and Anglo-Irish Literature* (San Antonio, Texas: Trinity University Press, 1976), pp. 113-115 [Primary and secondary books].

Lauterbach, Edward S., and W. Eugene Davis. *The Transitional Age: British Literature 1800-1920* (Troy, New York: Whitston Publishing Company, 1973), pp. 253-254 [Primary books. Secondary selected].

Longaker, Mark, and Edwin C. Bolles. *Contemporary English Literature* (New York: Appleton-Century-Crofts, 1953), pp. 61-62 [Primary books].

McCoy, Ralph E. "Manuscript Collections in Morris Library," *1 Carb S*, I, No. 2 (Spring-Summer 1974), pp. 153-162.

Mac Namara, Brinsley, ed. *Abbey Plays 1899-1948* (Dublin: At the Sign of the Three Candles, [1949]) [Productions at the Abbey Theatre].

Mellown, Elgin W. *A Descriptive Catalogue of the Bibliographies of 20th Century British Poets, Novelists, and Dramatists* (Troy, New York: Whitston Publishing Company, 1978), p. 305 [Primary and secondary bibliographies].

Millett, Fred B. *Contemporary British Literature; A Critical Survey and 232 Author Bibliographies* (New York: Harcourt, Brace, 1935), pp. 441-442 [Primary books. Secondary selected].

Nicoll, Allardyce. *English Drama 1900-1930; The Beginnings of the Modern Period* (Cambridge: Cambridge University Press, 1973), p. 916 [First productions].

O'Neill, Michael J. *Lennox Robinson* (New York: Twayne Publishers, 1964), pp. 15-21 [Primary books and plays]; pp. 181-184 [Secondary annotated].

Salem, James M. *A Guide to Critical Review. Part III: British and Continental Drama from Ibsen to Pinter* (Metuchen, New Jersey: Scarecrow Press, 1968), pp. 201-203 [Secondary selected].

Samples, Gordon. *The Drama Scholars' Index to Plays and Filmscripts; A Guide to Plays and Filmscripts in Selected Anthologies, Series and Periodicals* (Metuchen, New Jersey: Scarecrow Press, 1974), p. 324 [Primary selected].

Spinner, Kaspar. *Die Alte Dame Saget: Nein! Drei Irische Dramatiker. Lennox Robinson. Sean O'Casey. Denis*

Johnston (Bern: Francke, 1961), pp. 207-208 [Primary books and plays].

Temple, Ruth Z., and Martin Tucker. *Twentieth Century British Literature; A Reference Guide and Bibliography* (New York: Frederick Ungar, 1968), p. 223 [Primary books. Secondary selected].

Watson, George, ed. *The New Cambridge Bibliography of English Literature, Vol. 3: 1800-1900* (Cambridge: Cambridge University Press, 1969), columns 1943-1944 [Primary books. Secondary selected].

RUSSELL, George William [A. E.] (1867-1935)

Carens, James F. "A. E. (George W. Russell)," *Anglo-Irish Literature; A Review of Research*, ed. Richard J. Finneran (New York: Modern Language Association, 1976), pp. 446-452 [Secondary annotated].

Coleman, Arthur, and Gary R. Tyler. *Drama Criticism, Vol. I: A Checklist of Interpretation Since 1940 of English and American Plays* (Denver, Colorado: Alan Swallow, 1966), p. 19 [Secondary selected].

Denson, Alan. *Printed Writings by George William Russell (AE); A Bibliography with Some Notes on His Pictures and Portraits* (Evanston, Illinois: Northwestern University Press, 1961) [Primary]; pp. 182-205 [Secondary selected].

Kersnowski, Frank L., C. W. Spinks, and Laird Loomis. *A Bibliography of Modern Irish and Anglo-Irish Literature* (San Antonio, Texas: Trinity University Press, 1976), pp. 116-117 [Secondary books].

Kindilien, Caroline T. "George William Russell ('AE') and the Colby Collection," *Colby Library Quarterly*, IV (May 1955), pp. 21-24, 31-55.

Lauterbach, Edward S., and W. Eugene Davis. *The Transitional Age: British Literature 1800-1920* (Troy, New York: Whitston Publishing Company, 1973), pp. 257-258 [Primary books. Secondary selected].

Longaker, Mark, and Edwin C. Bolles. *Contemporary English Literature* (New York: Appleton-Century-Crofts, 1953), pp. 43-45 [Primary books. Secondary selected].

[Mac Manus, M. J.]. "Bibliographies of Irish Authors, No. 1 'AE'," *The Dublin Magazine*, V, No. 1 (January-March 1930), pp. 44-52 [Primary books annotated]. See "Additions," X, No. 4 (October-December 1935), pp. 74-76.

Mac Namara, Brinsley, ed. *Abbey Plays 1899-1948* (Dublin: At the Sign of the Three Candles, [1949]) [Productions at the Abbey Theatre].

Mellown, Elgin W. *A Descriptive Catalogue of the Bibliographies of 20th Century British Poets, Novelists, and Dramatists* (Troy, New York: Whitston Publishing Company, 1978), pp. 312-313 [Primary and secondary bibliographies].

Millett, Fred B. *Contemporary British Literature; A Critical Survey and 232 Author Bibliographies* (New York: Harcourt, Brace, 1935), pp. 446-448 [Primary books. Secondary selected].

Nicoll, Allardyce. *English Drama 1900-1930; The Beginnings of the Modern Period* (Cambridge: Cambridge University Press, 1973), p. 925 [First productions].

Temple, Ruth Z., and Martin Tucker. *Twentieth Century British Literature; A Reference Guide and Bibliography* (New York: Frederick Ungar, 1968), pp. 225-226 [Primary books. Secondary selected].

Watson, George, ed. *The New Cambridge Bibliography of English Literature, Vol. 3: 1800-1900* (Cambridge: Cambridge University Press, 1969), columns 1912-1916 [Primary books. Secondary selected].

SEARS, David (-   )

Hogan, Robert. *After the Irish Renaissance; A Critical History of the Irish Drama Since 'The Plough and the Stars'* (Minneapolis: University of Minnesota Press, 1967; London: Macmillan, 1968), p. 270 [Primary books.   Secondary selected] .

Nicoll, Allardyce. *English Drama 1900-1930; The Beginnings of the Modern Period* (Cambridge: Cambridge University Press, 1973), p. 937 [First productions] .

SHAW, George Bernard (1856-1950)

Adelman, Irving, and Rita Dworkin. *Modern Drama; A Checklist of Critical Literature on 20th Century Plays* (Metuchen, New Jersey: Scarecrow Press, 1967), pp. 264-289 [Secondary selected] .

Bosworth, R. F.   "Shaw Recordings at the B. B. C.," *Shaw Review,* VII (May 1964), pp. 42-46 [An essay describing ten recordings] .

Breed, Paul F., and Florence M. Sniderman. *Dramatic Criticism Index; A Bibliography of Commentaries on Playwrights from Ibsen to the Avant-Garde* (Detroit, Michigan: Gale Reserach Company, 1972), pp. 605-606 [Secondary selected] .

Broad, C. Lewis, and Violet M. Broad. *Dictionary to the Plays and Novels of Bernard Shaw, with Bibliography of His Works and of the Literature Concerning Him, with a Record of the Principal Shavian Play Productions* (London: A. and C. Black: New York: Macmillan, 1929), pp. 87-100 [Chronological list of primary books] ; pp.

101-112 [Chronological lists of other writings and of reported speeches] ; pp. 209-231 [Play productions] .

Coleman, Arthur, and Gary R. Tyler. *Drama Criticism, Vol. I: A Checklist of Interpretation Since 1940 of English and American Plays* (Denver, Colorado: Alan Swallow, 1966), pp. 186-195 [Secondary selected] .

Cutler, Bradley D., and Villa Stiles. *Modern British Authors; Their First Editions* (Greenberg: G. Allen, 1930; Folcroft, Pennsylvania: Folcroft Press, 1969), pp. 125-131 [Primary] .

Farley, Earl, and Marvin Carlson. "George Bernard Shaw: A Selected Bibliography (1945-1955)," *Modern Drama*, II, No. 2 (September 1959), pp. 188-202 [Secondary books] ; II, No. 3 (December 1959), pp. 295-325 [Secondary periodicals] .

Hartnoll, Phyllis. *Who's Who in Shaw* (London: Hamish Hamilton, 1975) [Alphabetical guide to the characters] .

Hugo, Leon. *Bernard Shaw; Playwright and Preacher* (London: Methuen, 1971), pp. 251-263 [Primary and secondary selected] .

Keough, Lawrence C. "George Bernard Shaw, 1946-1955: A Selected Bibliography," *Bulletin of Bibliography*, XXII (September-December 1959), pp. 224-226; XXIII (January-April 1960), pp. 20-24, XXIII (May-August 1960), pp. 36-41 [Primary and secondary] .

Laurence, Dan is working on a 2-volume bibliography of Shaw [Primary] .

Lauterbach, Edward S., and W. Eugene Davis. *The Transitional Age: British Literature 1880-1920* (Troy, New York: Whitston Publishing Company, 1973), pp. 264-268 [Primary books. Secondary selected] .

Lewis, Arthur O., Jr., and Stanley Weintraub. "Bernard Shaw—Aspects and Problems of Research," *Shaw Review*, III (1960), pp. 18-26 [Survey of secondary bibliogra-

phies] .

Lindblad, Ishrat. *Creative Evolution and Shaw's Dramatic Art* (Uppsala: Uppsala University, 1971), pp. 122-130 [Primary and secondary selected] .

Lowenstein, F. E. *The Rehearsal Copies of Bernard Shaw's Plays* (London: Reinhardt and Evans, 1950) [Primary. Extensive bibliographical, textual, and historical notes] .

Mac Namara, Brinsley, ed. *Abbey Plays 1899-1948* (Dublin: At the Sign of the Three Candles, [1949]) [Productions at the Abbey Theatre] .

Mellown, Elgin W. *A Descriptive Catalogue of the Bibliographies of 20th Century British Poets, Novelists, and Dramatists* (Troy, New York: Whitston Publishing Company, 1978), pp. 321-324 [Primary and secondary bibliographies] .

Milliken, Clara A. "Reading List of Modern Dramatists. . . Shaw," *Bulletin of Bibliography*, V (October 1907), pp. 52-53 [Secondary] .

Nicoll, Allardyce. *English Drama 1900-1930; The Beginnings of the Modern Period* (Cambridge: Cambridge University Press, 1973), pp. 941-943 [First productions] .

Palmer, Helen H., and Anne Jane Dyson. *European Drama Criticism* (Hamden, Connecticut: Shoe String Press, 1968), pp. 368-388; *Supplement* I (1970), pp. 157-162; *Supplement* II (1974), pp. 141-148 [Secondary selected] .

Pfeiffer, John, Elsie B. Adams, and Donald C. Haberman are working on a 3-volume bibliography of Shaw [Secondary annotated] .

Salem, James M. *A Guide to Critical Reviews. Part III: British and Continental Drama from Ibsen to Pinter* (Metuchen, New Jersey: Scarecrow Press, 1968), pp. 213-235 [Secondary selected] .

Samples, Gordon. *The Drama Scholars' Index to Plays and Filmscripts; A Guide to Plays and Filmscripts in Selected Anthologies, Series and Periodicals* (Metuchen, New Jersey: Scarecrow Press, 1974), p. 350 [Primary selected].

Shaw Bulletin, I-II (1951-1959). Title changed to *Shaw Review,* III (1960-to date). Almost every issue contains "A Continuing Check-List of Shaviana" by various editors [Primary and secondary].

Smith, Winifred. "Bernard Shaw and His Critics (1892-1938)," *Poet Lore,* XLVII (1941), pp. 76-83 [Secondary selected].

Spencer, T. J. "An Annotated Check-List of Criticism of the post-*Saint Joan* Plays," *Shaw Review,* II (1959), pp. 45-48 [Secondary selected].

Temple, Ruth Z., and Martin Tucker. *Twentieth Century British Literature: A Reference Guide and Bibliography* (New York: Frederick Ungar, 1968), pp. 229-230 [Primary books. Secondary selected].

Ward, Alfred C. *Bernard Shaw.* Writers and Their Work, I (London: Longmans, Green, 1951), pp. 41-56 [Primary].

Weintraub, Stanley. "Bernard Shaw," *Anglo-Irish Literature; A Review of Research,* ed. Richard J. Finneran (New York: Modern Language Association, 1976), pp. 167-215 [Secondary annotated].

Wells, Geoffrey H. *A Bibliography of the Books and Pamphlets of George Bernard Shaw* (London: Bookman's Journal, 1928). Reprinted from *The Bookman's Journal,* No. 11 (March 1925); No. 12 (April 1925) [Primary books].

SHIELS, George [George Morshiel] (1886-1949)

Breed, Paul F., and Florence M. Sniderman. *Dramatic Criticism Index; A Bibliography of Commentaries on Playwrights from Ibsen to the Avant-Garde* (Detroit, Michigan: Gale Research Company, 1972), pp. 661-662 [Secondary selected].

Hogan, Robert. *After the Irish Renaissance; A Critical History of the Irish Drama Since 'The Plough and the Stars'* (Minneapolis: University of Minnesota Press, 1967; London: Macmillan, 1968), p. 270 [Primary books] ; pp. 33-39 [Criticism].

Mac Namara, Brinsley, ed. *Abbey Plays 1899-1948* (Dublin: At the Sign of the Three Candles, [1949]) [Productions at the Abbey Theatre].

Mellown, Elgin W. *A Descriptive Catalogue of the Bibliographies of 20th Century British Poets, Novelists, and Dramatists* (Troy, New York: Whitston Publishing Company, 1978), p. 326 [Primary and secondary bibliographies].

Nicoll, Allardyce. *English Drama 1900-1930; The Beginnings of the Modern Period* (Cambridge: Cambridge University Press, 1973), p. 946 [First productions].

Sahal, N. *Sixty Years of Realistic Irish Drama (1900-1960)* (Bombay: Macmillan, 1971), pp. 120-133 [Plays and criticism].

Salem, James M. *A Guide to Critical Review. Part III: British and Continental Drama from Ibsen to Pinter* (Metuchen, New Jersey: Scarecrow Press, 1968), pp. 236-237 [Secondary selected].

Willison, I. R., ed. *The New Cambridge Bibliography of English Literature, Vol. 4: 1900-1950* (Cambridge: Cambridge University Press, 1972), columns 979-980 [Primary].

STEPHENS, James (1882-1950)

Bramsbäck, Birgit. *James Stephens; A Literary and Bibliographical Study* (Uppsala: Irish Institute of Uppsala University, 1959), pp. 57-209 [Primary and secondary bibliography].

Carens, James F. "James Stephens," *Anglo-Irish Literature, A Review of Research,* ed. Richard J. Finneran (New York: Modern Language Association, 1976), pp. 459-469 [Secondary annotated].

Cary, Richard, "James Stephen at Colby College," *Colby Library Quarterly,* V, No. 9 (March 1961), pp. 242-252.

"The James Stephens Papers [at Kent State University Library] ; A Catalogue," *The Serif,* II, No. 2 (1965), pp. 29-32.

Mac Namara, Brinsley, ed. *Abbey Plays 1899-1948* (Dublin: At the Sign of the Three Candles, [1949]) [Productions at the Abbey Theatre].

Mellown, Elgin W. *A Descriptive Catalogue of the Bibliographies of 20th Century British Poets, Novelists, and Dramatists* (Troy, New York: Whitston Publishing Company, 1978), pp. 340-341 [Primary and secondary bibliographies].

Pyle, Hilary. *James Stephens; His Work and an Account of His Life* (London: Routledge and Kegan Paul, 1965), pp. 183-190 [Primary] ; pp. 190-191 [Secondary selected].

Willison, I. R., ed. *The New Cambridge Bibliography of English Literature, Vol. 4: 1900-1950* (Cambridge: Cambridge University Press, 1972), columns 360-362 [Primary books. Secondary selected].

SYNGE, John Millington (1871-1909)

Adelman, Irving, and Rita Dworkin. *Modern Drama; A Checklist of Critical Literature on 20th Century Plays* (Metuchen, New Jersey: Scarecrow Press, 1967), pp. 306-309 [Secondary selected].

Babler, O. F. "John Millington Synge in Czech Translations," *Notes and Queries,* CXCI (21 September 1946), pp. 123-124 [Primary].

Bateson, F. W., ed. "John Millington Synge," *The Cambridge Bibliography of English Literature* (Cambridge: Cambridge University Press, 1940), vol. III, columns 1062-1063; *Supplement* (Cambridge: Cambridge University Press, 1957), columns 704-705 [Primary books. Secondary selected].

Bourgeois, Maurice. *John Millington Synge and the Irish Theatre* (London: Constable, 1913; New York: Benjamin Blom, 1965), pp. 251-265 [Primary]; pp. 265-296 [Secondary].

Breed, Paul F., and Florence M. Sniderman. *Dramatic Criticism Index; A Bibliography of Commentaries on Playwrights from Ibsen to the Avant-Garde* (Detroit, Michigan: Gale Research Company, 1972), pp. 685-693 [Secondary selected].

Bushrui, S. B. "A Select Bibliography," *Sunshine and the Moon's Delight: A Centenary Tribute to John Millington Synge 1871-1909* (Gerrard Cross, Bucks: Colin Smythe; Beirut: The American University, 1972), pp. 317-338 [Secondary].

Coleman, Arthur, and Gary R. Tyler. *Drama Criticism. Vol. I: A Checklist of Interpretation Since 1940 of English and American Plays* (Denver, Colorado: Alan Swallow, 1966), pp. 202-205 [Secondary selected].

Dysinger, Robert E. "The John Millington Synge Collection at Colby Library," *Colby Library Quarterly*, IV (February 1957), pp. 166-172; "Additions," pp. 192-194.

Estill, Adelaide Duncan. "Bibliography," *The Sources of Synge* (Philadelphia: University of Pennsylvania, 1939), pp. 42-51.

Gerstenberger, Donna. *John Millington Synge* (New York: Twayne Publishers, 1964), pp. 142-147 [Primary]; pp. 147-152 [Secondary annotated].

Greene, David H. "An Adequate Text of J. M. Synge," *Modern Language Notes*, LXI (November 1946), pp. 466-467 [Primary].

—, and E. M. Stephens. *John Millington Synge, 1871-1909* (New York: Macmillan, 1959), pp. 308-310 "A List of the Published Writings of Synge" [Books and contributions to periodicals].

Kersnowski, Frank L., C. W. Spinks, and Laird Loomis. *A Bibliography of Modern Irish and Anglo-Irish Literature* (San Antonio, Texas: Trinity University Press, 1976), pp. 131-134 [Secondary books].

Lauterbach, Edward S., and W. Eugene Davis. *The Transitional Age: British Literature 1880-1920* (Troy, New York: Whitston Publishing Company, 1973), pp. 284-285 [Primary books. Secondary selected].

Levitt, Paul. *J. M. Synge: A Bibliography of Published Criticism* (Dublin: Irish University Press, 1974) [Secondary].

Longaker, Mark, and Edwin C. Bolles. *Contemporary English Literature* (New York: Appleton-Century-Crofts, 1953), pp. 53-57 [Primary books. Secondary selected].

McGirr, Alice Thurston. "Reading List on John Millington Synge," *Bulletin of Bibliography*, VII (April 1913), pp. 114-115 [Secondary].

MacManus, M. J. "Bibliographies of Irish Authors No. 4:

John Millington Synge," *The Dublin Magazine*, V, No. 4 (October-December 1930), pp. 47-51 [Primary].

Mac Namara, Brinsley, ed. *Abbey Plays 1899-1948* (Dublin: At the Sign of the Three Candles, [1949]) [Productions at the Abbey Theatre].

MacPhail, Ian. "John Millington Synge: Some Bibliographical Notes," *Irish Book*, I (Spring 1959), pp. 3-10 [Surveys the bibliographical problems connected with Synge].

—, and M. Pollard. *John Millington Synge 1871-1909: A Catalogue of an Exhibition Held at Trinity College Library Dublin on the Occasion of the Fiftieth Anniversary of His Death* (Dublin: Dolmen Press, 1959) [Books, with bibliographical notes. List of periodical contributions, annotated. List of MSS].

Mellown, Elgin W. *A Descriptive Catalogue of the Bibliographies of 20th Century British Poets, Novelists, and Dramatists* (Troy, New York: Whitston Publishing Company, 1978), pp. 350-352 [Primary and secondary bibliographies].

Michie, Donald M. "Synge and His Critics," *Modern Drama*, XV, No. 4 (March 1973), pp. 427-432 [Secondary].

Mikhail, E. H. "Sixty Years of Synge Criticism, 1907-1967; A Selective Bibliography," *Bulletin of Bibliography*, XXVII, No. 1 (January-March 1970), pp. 11-13; XXVII, No. 2 (April-June 1970), pp. 53-56 [Secondary].

—. *J. M. Synge; A Bibliography of Criticism* (London: Macmillan, 1975) [Secondary].

Nicoll, Allardyce. *English Drama 1900-1930; The Beginnings of the Modern Period* (Cambridge: Cambridge University Press, 1973), p. 979 [First productions].

O'Hegarty, P. S. "Some Notes on the Bibliography of J. M. Synge, Supplement to Bourgeois and MacManus," *The Dublin Magazine*, XVII (January-March 1942), pp. 56-58

[Primary].

—. "Bibliographical Notes: The Abbey Theatre Wolfhound Series of Plays," *The Dublin Magazine,* XXII (April-June 1947), pp. 41-42 [Primary].

Palmer, Helen H., and Anne Jane Dyson. *European Drama Criticism* (Hamden, Connecticut: Shoe String Press, 1968), pp. 407-410; *Supplement* I (1970), pp. 171-172; *Supplement* II (1974), pp. 156-158 [Secondary selected].

Price, Alan. *Synge and Anglo-Irish Drama* (London: Methuen, 1961), pp. 229-231 [Secondary].

Saddlemyer, Ann. "Description of Textual Sources," appended to *J. M. Synge: Collected Works, Vols. III and IV* (London: Oxford University Press, 1968) [Primary].

—. " 'Infinite Riches in a Little Room'—The Manuscripts of John Millington Synge," *Long Room* (Dublin), I, No. 3 (Spring 1971), pp. 23-31 [Primary].

Salem, James M. *A Guide to Critical Reviews. Part III: British and Continental Drama from Ibsen to Pinter* (Metuchen, New Jersey: Scarecrow Press, 1968), pp. 244-246 [Secondary selected].

Samples, Gordon. *The Drama Scholars' Index to Plays and Filmscripts; A Guide to Plays and Filmscripts in Selected Anthologies, Series and Periodicals* (Metuchen, New Jersey: Scarecrow Press, 1974), pp. 375-376 [Primary selected].

The Synge Manuscripts in the Library of Trinity College Dublin (Dublin: Trinity College, 1971) [Primary].

Temple, Ruth Z., and Martin Tucker. *Twentieth Century British Literature: A Reference Guide and Bibliography* (New York: Frederick Ungar, 1968), pp. 239-240 [Primary books].

Thornton, Weldon. "J. M. Synge," *Anglo-Irish Literature; A*

Review of Research, ed. Richard J. Finneran (New York: Modern Language Association, 1976), pp. 315-365 [Secondary annotated].

Triesch, Manfred. "Some Unpublished J. M. Synge Papers," *English Language Notes,* IV, No. 1 (September 1966), pp. 49-51 [Primary].

Trinity College Dublin, "A Checklist of First Editions of Works by John Millington Synge and George William Russell," *T. C. D. Annual Bulletin* (1956), pp. 4-9.

Watson, George, ed. *The New Cambridge Bibliography of English Literature, Vol. 3: 1800-1900* (Cambridge: Cambridge University Press, 1969), columns 1934-1938 [Primary books. Secondary selected].

Zydler, Tomasz. "John Millington Synge and the Irish Theatre," *Kwartalnik Neofilologiczny* (Warsaw), XVIII (1971), pp. 383-396 [Secondary selected].

THOMPSON, Sam (1916-1965)

Hogan, Robert. "The Modern Drama," *Anglo-Irish Literature: A Review of Research,* ed. Richard J. Finneran (New York: Modern Language Association, 1976), p. 549 [Primary. Secondary selected].

TOMELTY, Joseph (1911-   )

Gracey, James W. "Joseph Tomelty: An Introductory Bibliography," *Irish Booklore* (1971), pp. 226-234 [Primary. Secondary selected].

Hogan, Robert. *After the Irish Renaissance; A Critical His-*

tory of the Irish Drama Since 'The Plough and the Stars' (Minneapolis: University of Minnesota Press, 1967; London: Macmillan, 1968), pp. 270-271 [Primary books] ; pp. 105-108 [Criticism] .

Mac Namara, Brinsley, ed. *Abbey Plays 1899-1948* (Dublin: At the Sign of the Three Candles, [1949]) [Productions at the Abbey Theatre] .

Sahal, N. *Sixty Years of Realistic Irish Drama (1900-1960)* (Bombay: Macmillan, 1971), pp. 169-176 [Plays and criticism] .

WALL, Mervyn (1908-   )

Hogan, Robert. "Bibliography," *Mervyn Wall* (Lewisburg, Pennsylvania: Bucknell University Press, 1972), pp. 74-75 [Primary. Secondary selected] .

Mac Namara, Brinsley, ed. *Abbey Plays 1899-1948* (Dublin: At the Sign of the Three Candles, [1949]) [Productions at the Abbey Theatre] .

Mellown, Elgin W. *A Descriptive Catalogue of the Bibliographies of 20th Century British Poets, Novelists, and Dramatists* (Troy, New York: Whitston Publishing Company, 1978), pp. 370-371 [Primary and secondary bibliographies] .

YEATS, Jack B. (1871-1957)

Breed, Paul F., and Florence M. Sniderman. *Dramatic Criticism Index; A Bibliography of Commentaries on Playwrights from Ibsen to the Avant-Garde* (Detroit, Michigan: Gale Research Company, 1972), p. 762 [Secondary selected] .

Caldwell, Martha. "A Chronology of Major Personal Events, Publications and Exhibitions" and "A Bibliography of the Published Writings," *Jack B. Yeats; A Centenary Gathering,* ed. Roger Mc Hugh (Dublin: Dolmen Press, 1971), pp. 107-109 and 110 114.

Hogan, Robert. *After the Irish Renaissance; A Critical History of the Irish Drama Since 'The Plough and the Stars'* (Minneapolis: University of Minnesota Press, 1967; London: Macmillan, 1968), p. 271 [Primary books] ; pp. 43-44 [Criticism] .

—. "The Modern Drama," *Anglo-Irish Literature: A Review of Research,* ed. Richard J. Finneran (New York: Modern Language Association, 1976), pp. 536-537 [Primary. Secondary selected] .

MacC[arvill] , E. "Jack B. Yeats: His Books," *The Dublin Magazine,* NS XX (July-September 1945), pp. 47-52 [Primary books and broadsheets] .

Mac Namara, Brinsley, ed. *Abbey Plays 1899-1948* (Dublin: At the Sign of the Three Candles, [1949]) [Productions at the Abbey Theatre] .

Mellown, Elgin W. *A Descriptive Catalogue of the Bibliographies of 20th Century British Poets, Novelists, and Dramatists* (Troy, New York: Whitston Publishing Company, 1978), pp. 395-396 [Primary and secondary bibliographies] .

Pyle, Hilary. *Jack B. Yeats; A Biography* (London: Routledge and Kegan Paul, 1970), pp. [175]-180 [Primary] .

Samples, Gordon. *The Drama Scholars' Index to Plays and Filmscripts; A Guide to Plays and Filmscripts in Selected Anthologies, Series and Periodicals* (Metuchen, New Jersey: Scarecrow Press, 1974), p. 426 [Primary selected] .

Skelton, Robin. *The Collected Plays of Jack B. Yeats* (London: Secker & Warburg, 1971), pp. 377-378 [First productions].

Sligo County Library and Museum. *Jack B. Yeats and His Family* (Sligo: Sligo County Library and Museum, 1971) [A catalogue of the exhibition held 29 October-29 December 1971].

YEATS, William Butler (1865-1939)

Adams, Hazard. "Yeats Scholarship and Criticism: A Review of Research," *Texas Studies in Literature and Language,* III (Winter 1962), pp. 439-451 [Essay-survey of primary material and secondary writings].

Adelman, Irving, and Rita Dworkin. *Modern Drama; A Checklist of Critical Literature on 20th Century Plays* (Metuchen, New Jersey: Scarecrow Press 1967), pp. 332-340 [Secondary selected].

Black, Hester M. *William Butler Yeats: A Catalog of an Exhibition from the P. S. O'Hegarty Collection in the University of Kansas Library* (Lawrence, Kansas: University of Kansas Library, 1958).

Breed, Paul F., and Florence M. Sniderman. *Dramatic Criticism Index; A Bibliography of Commentaries on Playwrights from Ibsen to the Avant-Garde* (Detroit, Michigan: Gale Research Company, 1972), pp. 762-776 [Secondary selected].

Coleman, Arthur, and Gary R. Tyler. *Drama Criticism, Vol. I: A Checklist of Interpretation Since 1940 of English and American Plays* (Denver, Colorado: Alan Swallow, 1966), pp. 232-235 [Secondary selected].

Cross, K. G. W. "The Fascination of What's Difficult: A Survey of Yeats Criticism and Research," in *In Excited Reverie: A Centenary Tribute to William Butler Yeats, 1865-1939,* ed. A. Norman Jeffares and K. G. W. Cross

(London and New York: Macmillan, 1965), pp. 315-
337 [Essay on the history of Yeats scholarship].

—, and R. T. Dunlop. *A Bibliography of Yeats Criticism,
1887-1965* (London: Macmillan, 1971) [Secondary].

Cutler, Bradley D., and Villa Stiles. *Modern British Authors;
Their First Editions* (Greenberg: G. Allen, 1930; Fol-
croft, Pennsylvania: Folcroft Press, 1969), pp. 164-167
[Primary].

Dougan, R. O., comp. *W. B. Yeats: Manuscripts and Printed
Books Exhibited in the Library of Trinity College, Dublin* (Dublin: At the Sign of the Three Candles, 1956)
[Primary]. To be supplemented by "Books and Manuscripts of W. B. Yeats," *The Times Literary Supplement*
(4 May 1956), p. 276.

Durkan, Michael J. *William Butler Yeats 1865-1965: A Catalogue of His Works and Associated Items in Olin Library, Wesleyan University* (Middleton, Connecticut:
Olin Memorial Library; Dublin: Dolmen Press, 1965).

Finneran, Richard J. "W. B. Yeats," *Anglo-Irish Literature:
A Review of Research* (New York: Modern Language
Association, 1976), pp. 216-314 [Secondary annotated].

Gerstenberger, Donna. "Yeats and the Theater: A Selected
Bibliography," *Modern Drama,* VI, No. 1 (May 1963),
pp. 64-71 [Secondary selected and annotated].

Jochum, K. P. S. *W. B. Yeats's Plays; An Annotated Checklist of Criticism* (Saarbrücken: Anglistisches Institut der
Universitat des Saarlandes, 1966) [Secondary].

— has completed *W. B. Yeats: A Classified Bibliography of
Criticism Including Additions to Allan Wade's 'Bibliogra-
phy of the Writings of W. B. Yeats' and a Section on the
Irish Literary and Dramatic Revival.*

Kersnowski, Frank L., C. W. Spinks, and Laird Loomis. *A
Bibliography of Modern Irish and Anglo-Irish Literature*
(San Antonio, Texas: Trinity University Press, 1976),

pp. 145-156 [Secondary books] .

Lauterbach, Edward S., and W. Eugene Davis. *The Transitional Age: British Literature 1880-1920* (Troy, New York: Whitston Publishing Company, 1973), pp. 307-311 [Primary books. Secondary selected] .

Longaker, Mark, and Edwin C. Bolles. *Contemporary English Literature* (New York: Appleton-Century-Crofts, 1953), pp. 35-43 [Primary books. Secondary selected] .

McGirr, Alice Thurston. "Reading List on William Butler Yeats," *Bulletin of Bibliography,* VII (1913), pp. 82-83 [Secondary annotated] .

Mac Namara, Brinsley, ed. *Abbey Plays 1899-1948* (Dublin: At the Sign of the Three Candles, [1949]) [Productions at the Abbey Theatre] .

Mellown, Elgin W. *A Descriptive Catalogue of the Bibliographies of 20th Century British Poets, Novelists, and Dramatists* (Troy, New York: Whitston Publishing Company, 1978), pp. 396-399 [Primary and secondary bibliographies] .

Nicoll, Allardyce. *English Drama 1900-1930; The Beginnings of the Modern Period* (Cambridge: Cambridge University Press, 1973), pp. 1043-1045 [First productions] .

O'Hegarty, P. S. "Notes on the Bibliography of W. B. Yeats," *The Dublin Magazine,* XIV (October-December 1939), pp. 61-65; XV (January-March 1940), pp. 37-42 [Primary] .

Oshima, Shotaro. "Bibliography of Yeats in Japan," *W. B. Yeats and Japan* (Tokyo: Hokuseido Press; London: Luzac, 1965), pp. 149-189 [Secondary] .

Palmer, Helen H., and Ann Jane Dyson. *European Drama Criticism* (Hamden, Connecticut: Shoe String Press, 1968), pp. 433-439; *Supplement* I (1970), pp. 185-188; *Supplement* II (1974), pp. 172-174 [Secondary selected] .

Roth, William M. *A Catalogue of English and American First Editions of William Butler* Yeats (New Haven, Connecticut: Yale University Press, 1939) [Prepared for an exhibition of his works at Yale University Library].

Salem, James M. *A Guide to Critical Reviews. Part III: British and Continental Drama from Ibsen to Pinter* (Metuchen, New Jersey: Scarecrow Press, 1968), p. 266 [Secondary selected].

Samples, Gordon. *The Drama Scholars' Index to Plays and Filmscripts; A Guide to Plays and Filmscripts in Selected Anthologies, Series and Periodicals* (Metuchen, New Jersey: Scarecrow Press, 1974), p. 426 [Primary selected].

Saul, George B. "Thread to a Labyrinth: A Selective Bibliography on Yeats," *Bulletin of the New York Public Library*, LVIII (1954), pp. 344-347 [A severely restricted list of books].

—. *Prolegomena to the Study of Yeats's Plays* (Philadelphia: University of Pennsylvania Press, 1958; rep. 1971) [Secondary].

Schwartz, Jacob. *1100 Obscure Points: The Bibliographies of 25 English and 21 American Authors* (Bristol, England: Chatford House Press, 1931; rep. 1969) [Primary].

Skene, Reg. *The Cuchulain Plays of W. B. Yeats; A Study* (London: Macmillan, 1974), pp. 265-271 [Primary and secondary selected].

Stoll, John E. *The Great Deluge: A Yeats Bibliography* (Troy, New York: The Whitston Publishing Company, 1971) [Primary and Secondary].

Symons, Arthur. *A Bibliography of the First Editions of Books by William Butler Yeats* (London: First Edition Club; New York: Bowker, 1924) [Primary].

Wade, Allan. *A Bibliography of the Writings of W. B. Yeats.* Soho Bibliographies No. 1. Third Edition, Revised and

Edited by Russell K. Alspach (London: Rubert Hart-Davis, 1968) [Primary. Secondary books]. Additions to Wade have been made by K. P. S. Jochum in *Bulletin of Bibliography* (1971); by Colton Johnson in *Notes and Queries* (1972); by Shirley W. Vinall in *Notes and Queries* (1973); by George Monteiro in *Notes and Queries* (1974); and by Colin Smythe in *Long Room* (1974).

William Butler Yeats, 1865-1939: Catalogue of an Exhibition, 13th-22nd May 1965 (Newcastle-upon-Tyne: University of Newcastle, 1965) [A short list].

INDEX

A) Index of Names

B) Index to Titles